SACRED COMMERCE

THE RISE OF THE GLOBAL CITIZEN

AYMAN SAWAF &
ROWAN GABRIELLE

Copyright © 2007, Ayman Sawaf and Rowan Gabrielle
Cover image: © iStockphoto.com, Duncan Walker

All rights reserved. No part of this book may be reproduced without written permission from the publisher.

This book is manufactured in the United States of America.

Cover design and illustrations: Heather Bowen

ISBN # 978-1-4679894-5-9

Sacred Commerce
P.O. Box 719
Ojai, CA 93024
Email: ayman@sacredcommerce.com
rowan@sacredcommerce.com
Website: www.sacredcommerce.com

First Printing December 2007

Acknowledgments

It seems that the more you awaken your creativity and manifest your dreams, the more people you want to thank.

First, we would like to thank Kevin Ryerson, who inspired this book in 1993 when we went with him on a trip to Egypt for our honeymoon. It was there, in the Temple of Isis, that knowledge of the Merchant Priesthood and their legacy first came to our attention.

Second, we would like to thank our friends Roger Housden and Geralyn Gendreau, both exceptional authors in their own right, who we would almost call our co-authors for having added so much. We are humbled by your eloquence and your skill, and are so grateful for what you have added to this project.

A big thank you to other friends that have contributed to this project in different ways: John Willis our editor for organizing everything, Heather Bowen for the beautiful cover and all the illustrations, Gayatri Roshan, Gabriel Cousens, Harold Bloomfield, Page Nolker, Norman Monson, Jach Pursel, and David Traub.

And finally a massive thank you to the people that sustain and nurture us, our family and close friends Halla, Aziz, Kareem, Paula, Nick, Udhayan, Joris, Temujin, Cody, Omar, Bashar, Jouhaina, Dickon, Teresa, Susu, Stacie, Khaled, Nouha, Jocelyn, and Dru; to Shirish, Joey, David and the Urth.TV team for their amazing commitment to being a living demonstration of Sacred Commerce; and to many, many others all around the world whom we treasure.

Gratefully,

Ayman and Rowan

Dedication

This book is dedicated to Nick Hart-Williams and Aziz Sawaf.

Table of Contents

Acknowledgments   iii
Dedication   iv
Introduction   vii

Part One: **Sacred Commerce**

The Rise of the Conscious Consumer   3

The Merchant Priesthood   9

The Gift   19

The 4th Bottom Line   29

Part Two: **The Journey of the Merchant Priesthood**

The Merchant Priesthood of the Ancient World   39

Initiation and Training   45

Origins, Legend, and Myth   51

The Merlin and Arthur Legacy
to Europe and the King's Court   63

The Prophet Mohammad's Part   69

The Knights Templar   73

Tulip Mania: The First Great Market Bubble   85

The Founding of America   91

Today's Knights of Commerce
The Rise of the Global Citizen   97

Part Three: **The Emotional Alchemist**

Emotional Intelligence   113

Emotional Alchemy   121

Partnership with the Pulse   133

Appreciation and Wonder:
Gateway to Beauty   139

Beauty, Goodness, and Truth:
The Eternal Verities   143

Introduction

This book is built on the Four Cornerstone model detailed in *Executive EQ: Emotional Intelligence in Leadership and Organizations.* We could easily have written another 400-page book, but we wanted to create a quick and magical read rather than another lengthy text full of facts, figures and statistics. Those were important in *Executive EQ*; our plan for this book is quite different. Our aim with this book is to tell you a beautiful and enchanting story—one that could very well change how we all do business. The storytellers in us encourage you to approach this book as you might a romantic novel, allowing the concepts and images to nurture and inspire you. This is not meant to be a factual account of history, although the stories contained herein may give you new insight into humanity's past and inspire you to "party-cipate," as we like to say, in the creation of a brilliant future.

This is the story of Sacred Commerce. It tells of the Merchant Priests whose unique ministry involved the skill of Emotional Alchemy and taught them to pursue the path of beauty. This lyrical look at evolution through the eyes of a grander plan began as a collaboration with our friend Kevin Ryerson who introduced us to the Merchant Priesthood and the "drop of joy" technique that is quintessential to the practice of Emotional Alchemy. Over the years the book went through many incarnations and partnerships as we collected the stories of Sacred Commerce. Although this book is a collaboration of many, it has been written in Ayman's voice. Sacred Commerce is designed to be one of the first of a new style of book we call 'living' or 'Wiki' books. This 2007 publication has just two authors and nine contributors who mostly have never met, but as we go forward we invite each and every one of you to become a co-author with us. You can go to www.sacredcommerce.com and participate by adding your stories and critique as together we further detail, refine, and put these concepts into practice. We will re-publish this book every year and include the most relevant and exciting additions, thus allowing the book to be continuously re created over the years to keep it fresh and relevant to the changing times. The concept and practice of "Sacred Commerce" will be given life and breath by you, allowing it to grow faster than if we tried to "own" or "lead" it ourselves. Every party-cipitant will be honored.

The Merchant Priests of old set the stage. They were followed by the Knights of Commerce, Renaissance men and woman all over the world in every culture and religion. Today, the baton is being passed once again. This is our story and you might find in it your story. The Merchant Priest/Priestess is awakening in all of us. Our dream is that Sacred Commerce will become a lifestyle, not just a business activity, and that the growing Global Citizen movement will grab hold of the baton of Sacred Commerce as one of its organizing principles.

The central principle and "engine" of culture is no longer religion or politics, as was the case in the past. Like it or not, commerce has become the primary force propelling our species and human society forward. We are witnessing a commerce-centric (r)evolution, a whole new form of 'conscious capitalism', wherein business transactions the world over will become the main conduit of social and cultural evolution.

In joy,

Ayman Sawaf and Rowan Gabrielle

Part One:
Sacred Commerce

The Rise of the Conscious Consumer

Nestled in the shadow of Mount Tam, just twenty minutes outside San Francisco, is the town of Mill Valley where my wife Rowan and I live halftime. Founded in 1896, some forty years before the Golden Gate Bridge was complete, this cozy little village was named after its primary commercial enterprise—the making of lumber from redwood trees. In the heart of town a bustling train station once buzzed with life as freshly cut lumber was carried off to San Francisco where the colorful redwood planks would deck the halls and the floors of many a "painted lady" Victorian. But these days the mill is silent, and the town no longer echoes with the sound of the saw.

Today the former train station is the Depot Plaza—a charming village center that often overspills with the sound of drums and laughter. Flanked by coffee shops, the plaza finds locals and visitors alike sitting or strolling, chatting or playing in the afternoon sun.

One block from the square, next door to the Sweetwater Saloon, is an 1800 square foot storefront that once was a health food store called Living Foods. Typical of stores of its ilk in the 70s and 80s, the small dark shop was often crowded with granola-loving types—those tree-huggers, Dead-heads, hippies and earth mama's whose fondness for natural foods could hardly be thought of as a force to be reckoned with. But a force they were, and the reckoning came.

In another part of the country two college dropouts heard the call of the future and opened their own living foods store. Spoofing the name of a large grocery chain, they called the store Safeway. Like most health food enterprises, Safeway was a small but growing concern. In no time at all the store began to bust its tie-dyed britches. Owners John and Renee did the best they could to keep the shelves well-stocked but, with little storage space at the store, boxes of whole grain cereal and organic what-not started to spill over into their apartment. When the landlord took an unfriendly stance toward this and booted the pair, they put their heads together and created a makeshift home at the back of their store. A Hobart dishwasher with a water hose became their shower stall. This humble renegade beginning eventually became America's first and still largest natural foods grocery chain: Whole Foods Markets.

John Mackey and Renee Lawson caught a groundswell that grew into a tidal wave of commercial interest in products related to health and wellbeing. In essence, they felt the pulse of a growing market that became such a force in our economy it demanded to be named. The acronym LOHAS stands for Lifestyles of Health and Sustainability and designates this 325 billion dollar a year market pioneered in the early 70s by entrepreneurs who saw the future in their use of the word *whole*. Whether we spell it Holistic or Wholistic, there is no way around the powerful force of an idea whose time had come. Planted in the fertile ground of post-60s optimism, the seed of wholeness began to grow.

If ever there were a title to summarize the passion of a generation, *The Holistic Health Handbook: a Tool for Attaining Wholeness of Body, Mind, and Spirit* would surely top the list as would the *Whole Earth Catalog,* an oversized newspaper-quality mail order tome.

When Alan Goldman, an event producer who had been working with the National Health Federation in New York, teamed up with publisher Joseph Cotler in the early 80s to launch their first Wholelife Expo, a template was created. Soon, that template would replicate and morph into a nomadic counterculture marketplace to showcase the emerging new business paradigm and the green economy, as illustrated by the success of many of the Body, Mind and Spirit genre of expositions and conferences, health shows and the Green Festival.

> **[Sidebar]** Since 1981, the Wholelife Expos and Conferences have been one of the early pioneers of the conscious commerce movement, offering expositions and conferences across the country where up to 20,000 people would gather around best-selling authors, cutting edge speakers, and hundreds of wholistic and green vendors to socialize, network, shop, learn, teach, and be entertained in a spirit of community and celebration. To many, the Wholelife Expos were the umbrella movement and the original conscious community network that incubated, promoted, and helped market hundreds of today's famous teachers, authors, and wholistic and green businesses. It has served over a million customers and over 10,000 teachers, practitioners, and vendors while successfully connecting the cultural creative communities.

Within a few short years this marketplace of "New Age" products and ideas caught on like a wildfire as alternative approaches to everything from how we eat to how we pray captured the imagination and the pocketbook of more and more of the mainstream. As this grassroots movement toward conscious consumerism grew, the list of products and services offered grew as well. The various events and expos that sprung up everywhere became a veritable thermometer for the purchasing power behind America's new age fever. Interest in healthy and ecological lifestyles, personal and spiritual development, alternative medicine, and all things esoteric now flourishes worldwide.

For nearly half a century prior to the emergence of this new paradigm, consumerism had been dominated by a value system that elevated science, industry and technology above all else. The industrial revolution and the age of technology set housewives free with electric appliances like dishwashers, refrigerators, and steam irons. The first telephones, radios, and television sets radically altered the atmosphere of the American home. Likewise, the assembly line, the steam engine, calculators, and eventually computers completely changed the work environment. It is easy to see the value system that governed product development during that period in the then-popular slogan "Better living through chemistry."

With hindsight we might be tempted to ask: *What in God's name were they thinking? Did we really think that chemistry and technology alone would do it?* And yet, it is important to keep the process of cultural evolution in mind to maintain a balanced perspective. Each new development in culture is a response to the limitations of the previous one; it is the very nature of a "counterculture" to adopt new values and lifestyle choices in an attempt to resolve the problems of the previous paradigm. Progress occurs through a cultural dialectic of thesis, antithesis, and synthesis. The postmodern sensitivity and value system expressed by the green movement emerged in direct response to the limitations of the post- industrial revolution.

The new paradigm in business grew out of the broken dream of technology-as-king. As awareness grew and we began to understand the deleterious impact of technology on the environment and our quality of life, conscious consumers began to rise up out of factory ashes. "Better to Live Green" is part of a natural progression of values that has inherent power and thus inspires a whole new mindset as well as a whole new market place.

In his book, *Cultural Creatives*, Dr. Paul Ray documents the rise of the conscious consumer. Germinated in the 1950s with the Beat Generation, beatniks became peaceniks and the flower children, and baby boomers of the sixties gave birth to a population boom with ever more conscious lifestyle choices. To supply the needs and wants of the conscious consumer, business had to adapt and change. More and more aware of the effect their actions had on the whole, conscious consumers wanted to know what a product was made of, where it was made, who made it, how it would affect them physically and emotionally, as well as how it would impact the environment.

As businesses responded to the demand of consumers, the new values expressed began to percolate and have an impact on how business was being done. The rise in consciousness began to influence management styles.

Over the last 20 years the green MBA movement has developed a business model that includes conscience and sustainability within commerce, ending up with what is known now as conscious commerce or sustainable businesses practices. The old paradigm wherein the bottom line return on investment (ROI) meant how much cash flowed back into the hands of investors gave way to the concept of the Triple Bottom Line (People, Planet, Profit). The rate of return on investment is no longer measured only in cold hard cash but in more humane and balanced terms—return to the employees who created the profit and return to the planet or the community at large. As of today, near 45% of the world's largest companies publish Triple Bottom Line reports. In these reports the returns to the planet and the employees mainly take the form of contributions to charitable causes and profit sharing/stock options to their employees.

In Australia, Westpac Bank recently issued an expanded approach to traditional accountability standards. They now measure their progress using three criteria: prosperity, social justice, and environment. Their recent corporate report (www.westpac.com.au) includes claims of ethical business, transparency, human rights, awareness of environmental concerns, caring for employees, and more. Suddenly the bottom line is not so simple – it has become the Triple Bottom Line. Organizations have their own survival issues and profit interests, but they live in a local and global community and are increasingly waking up to (or being forced to) become accountable to them.

This change has come about for a variety of reasons: (1) The changing values among stakeholders (the notion that multiple stakeholders define the organization, not just stockholders, but a combination of employees, managers, the larger community, and the environment itself), (2) The employees' desire for an organization that they can be proud of, and (3) The CEOs' value shifts, which have partly come about because of (a) personal internal contradictions such as heart attacks, cancer and other lifestyle diseases, as well as (b) external pressures such as looking out their windows and seeing angry protestors (often their own children).

This growing awareness and humane mindset clarifies our purchasing power and makes it possible to "vote with our dollar" in ways we never dreamed before the rise of the conscious consumer. Like all that came before, conscious consumerism is a step on the ladder of our collective evolution. In another 10 years or so we may see the rise of the Sacred Consumer, but that's another story.

The Merchant Priesthood

Born in a merchant family, I grew up in a business environment. Although I was fascinated by business from an early age, a nagging concern always accompanied the intrigue. At times the nagging would become outright irritation when I couldn't help but notice that commerce sometimes robbed rather than enriched humanity. Disillusioned by the arrogance and lack of sensitivity I saw in the majority of business people, I rebelled and decided to become an industrial engineer instead. After finishing college I wondered what I should I do with my degree. An industrial engineer was not my cup of tea and the love for commerce was still in my blood, despite my issues with it. So I decided to become an Entrepreneur.

In late 70s in the beautiful Arabian Wild West, I set myself up to experience the development of a region I was fascinated by. Sensing the need for lighting products in Saudi Arabia during one of its early construction booms, I spent the first ten years of my business career designing, manufacturing, and selling lights, spearheading one of the largest lighting companies in the Middle East with assembly lines in Europe and the Far East.

My life, however, was based solely on logic and reason with not so much as a single drop of magic. I knew nothing of spirituality or emotions; life for me was all about math, statistics, engineering and business. By my mid 30's I was in an early mid-life crisis, challenged on both home and health fronts and quite fed up with my life. On a kind of inner search to understand what was happening to me, I decided to spend some time alone. I took a trip to Thailand, and a number of strange coincidences triggered my interest in spiritual realities. Among other things I found myself watching a video of Shirley MacLaine. In one scene I saw an intuitive consultant named Kevin Ryerson advising Shirley on some of her business projects and her spiritual journey. Being in a crisis my interest instantly piqued, and I set out to find Kevin.

Impressed with Ryerson's credentials and detailed knowledge of mythology, religion, and Emotional Intelligence amongst many other subjects, I booked a few consultations (a) to understand the source of my depression and deep disappointment in life and (b) to find my way out of it, which I did in a relatively short period of time, predominantly through emotional healing and my discovery of Emotional Literacy. A period of accelerated growth found me implementing exercises and techniques to awaken the feminine and the sacred in me. My creativity and intuition began to blossom and my Emotional Intelligence started to percolate.

With my own head back above water, I found myself furious that we are not taught these most basic human skills in school. This sparked a passion inside me to share the power of Emotional Literacy with others, especially children. I called Kevin to discuss with him my new dream of creating the school of the future, a new model for elementary schools. This dream gave way instead to building a children's multi media company. Kevin and I became very good friends and spent countless hours and days developing the first Emotional Literacy curriculum in a series of books and related films.

[Sidebar] Soon after, with my wife and partner Rowan, we went on to create FEEL (the Foundation for Education in Emotional Literacy, www.feel.org). FEEL was founded in 1993 with a mission to ensure all children develop the vital life skills of Emotional Literacy. It was the first nonprofit of its kind, publishing an Emotional Literacy newsletter and distributing it to hundreds of thousands of teachers, psychology departments, universities, and schools. In the late 90's it merged with www.6seconds.org and has recently launched the "One Million Signature" campaign to lobby the U.S. government and the UN to bring Emotional Literacy into our educational system as the antidote to many of our society's ills and as the basic building block to being a happy and successful person.

My shift from the lighting business to the en-lightening business came through another catalytic meeting. As a part of my own healing journey, and expressing more of myself, I got into composing and playing music. I had just released my fourth album when a friend came to me saying that an associate of his had heard it and wanted to meet me. The man was Dr. Christopher Hills. I assumed Hills wanted to talk to me about an investment or business deal. After all, at that point in my life nobody ever sought me out to talk unless it was about business. I had left behind my old way of doing business to pursue music and the business of Emotional Literacy and I felt quite reluctant to take the meeting.

Dr Hills was tenacious and insisted we meet. When I looked at this striking man for the first time, I remember thinking he was some kind of Merlin or wizard. I could see the Christ light beaming in his eyes. Later I discovered he had written 22 books on spiritual philosophy and the science of consciousness. That meeting was an important turning point in my life. His way of doing business planted a seed that has since bloomed into the practice we would come to call "Sacred Commerce."

In her book *Megatrends 2010: The Rise of Conscious Capitalism*, Patricia Aburdene describes the present-day transformation of free enterprise by spiritual values. A trend tracker whose earlier bestseller *Megatrends 2000* foresaw the technology boom of the 90s, Aburdene states as "an economic truth" that spiritual values "like Trust and Integrity literally *translate* into revenue, profits and prosperity." Now, more than half a decade into the new millennium, she foresees—and verifies with story after story—a trend of remarkable courage and commitment among executives. Captains of industry the world over are relinquishing the old-school ways of greed and secrecy in favor of moderation and transparency as a new economy emerges wherein "money and morals thrive side by side."

Let's look at Dr. Christopher Hills' experience as an example of this shift. Hills traveled to India in the early 60s to pursue enlightenment. As part of his initiation he went walking from village to village with a begging bowl. He would often be swarmed by hundreds of starving children pressing their own begging bowls toward his dirty robes. As he entered one particular village he was literally swarmed by close to a hundred children. In that moment he looked up to God and promised to find a solution to famine.

Over the years he had occasion to meet many political and spiritual leaders in India. In an effort to take the science of yoga to the West, he initiated the first world yoga conference inviting the most prominent yogis in India to attend. But a power struggle ensued as the gurus battled over who would get the most airtime at the conference. Appalled by this behavior Hills began to notice an alarming paradox. According to custom and the culture in India, a guru's followers were encouraged to donate to their spiritual teacher and guide. Many of these gurus had millions of followers. Starving, bedraggled devotees—whose bone-thin children had to beg in the streets and often died of malnutrition before reaching adulthood—would hand their meager income over in the hope of being reborn to a more gracious life among an upper caste. It sadly reminded him of how most churches and organized religion in the West encourage their members to contribute a portion of their

Cell Tech Blue-Green Algae people doing here? I thought. *And how did they get this kid on board?*

I had no idea the Cell Tech folks were already in Europe, and I felt more than a little miffed. As the days progressed, I learned that this young woman named Rowan had been traveling back and forth to America since she was 15 working on environmental and business documentaries with her father and researching super food and nutrition. With no money, no business experience, and no serious backing, she had knocked on the door of Cell Tech in Oregon and convinced the owner to give her the exclusive agency for the UK with an option for the whole of Europe. She had already started her distributor downline and was going from place to place promoting financial health and nutritional wealth through conscious commerce.

In matter of a few months she and I formed a corporation to develop a series of joint projects together and eventually married. Thanks to Kevin Ryerson, we exchanged our vows inside Stonehenge.

An expert in mythology and history, Kevin had a specific interest in Egyptian myths and mysticism. A few months after he married Rowan and I. Kevin invited us to join a tour he was leading in Egypt. While in the Temple of Isis in Philae, the area known as "the jewel of the Nile," Rowan and I split off briefly from the group. She had stopped to change the film in her camera while I waited nearby. The rest of the group had followed Kevin; they were several hundred yards ahead of us. Suddenly two Egyptians men walked up and, speaking in broken English, asked if we wanted to take our picture by a nearby square stone with a figure carved on it. Thinking they were after a tip, and speaking Arabic very well, I replied, "No thank you." The two insisted and would not take no for an answer and kept following us. "We don't want money," one man said. "We want to take your picture; here, please, stand here," the other said, pointing to the square stone. Finally, in an effort to just get rid of them, we agreed to sit for a photograph. We stood beside the stone they had pointed to repeatedly and had our picture taken. They handed the camera back and disappeared.

On the way out, we told Kevin about the odd interaction involving the two men and showed him the stone where we had posed for the camera. He looked and said, "Ah, curious. But that is not just any stone. Look again. Do you see what this is?" We spoke together, saying: "No." Kevin said, "This is the Egyptian god Bes, the god of commerce. He is the god who oversees the Merchant Priesthood." We both smiled and looked at each other, filled with curiosity and wonder. "Merchant Priesthood?" I'd never heard of a merchant priest; I had known that there were temple priests and celebration priests and healing priests. But a merchant priest? I was aware too that the Pope often appointed one of the bishops to handle the business dealings of the Vatican as well as merchant affairs, so the idea did not strike me as too far-fetched.

Over time Kevin began to tell us stories of the Merchant Priesthood. Throughout the next several years we did a good bit of research and gathered anecdotal evidence from a variety of sources; we will review those stories in detail in Part Two. Having found a number of references that confirmed the idea that a Merchant Priesthood had indeed existed, we traveled around the world to various sacred sites, exploring and researching these stories.

What fascinated me from the start was the idea that commerce could be a vehicle to raise consciousness as well as a spiritual path towards self-realization. Could commerce, that intrinsic and basic function of exchanging goods and services, actually lift a culture to a level of sacredness that might otherwise not be attained, as well as putting those who practiced it on an accelerated growth trajectory? This idea made perfect sense to me and rang through my mind like a clarifying bell.

The Gift

Revered as a spiritual path, commerce emerged long ago as a tool to advance mankind. Among the Merchant Priesthood of old Egypt it was viewed as a gift from god/goddess, sacred and balanced by its very nature. It was seen as a solution or a map to deal with the issues of survival, security and community, and as an ally in our process of conscious evolution when we are ready to undertake that ultimate spiritual adventure of all: Coming home.

All cultures have this going out and coming back as a central theme in their mythology. We leave Paradise, our sense of oneness with God, and get lost in the wilderness, separated and apart from God. However, we are always given a map and the free will to eventually come back. Whether we seek salvation, enlightenment, or the Promised Land, we are all involved in a similar process of coming back home to God. Joseph Campbell named this essential archetypal pattern "the heroes' journey." Below is a graph that summarizes the many maps or psychological models using a rendition of Abraham Maslow's Hierarchy of Needs pyramid.

The concept, simply put, is that human beings start by meeting or fulfilling their needs from the bottom up. As we meet the needs of survival and security a sense of happiness emerges and stretches us to pursue the higher needs of community/belonging, esteem, expression, knowing, and beauty.

The Hierarchy of Needs

- Spirituality/self-realization/aesthetics
- Vision, knowing, understanding
- The expression of creativity/productivity
- Esteem/loving relationships
- Community/belonging
- Safety/security
- Survival

Let's look closely at the gift of Commerce and how it can lead both the individual and society **to prosperity, peace, and conscious evolution.**

First and foremost, one of the greatest known gifts of commerce is Abundance with its ability to lift people out of poverty and the needs of survival and security. This is so evident in our society and history there is no need to expand on it. By reducing the pain and suffering of the constant struggle just to survive, abundance opens the door to other avenues of expression such as relationships, creativity, and the pursuit of happiness and spirituality. "Abundance" is defined as having access to the resources you need, at the time you need them. It has nothing to do with stockpiling money or assets. In the context of Sacred Commerce, the emphasis of the gift turns to the enjoyment and the sharing of that abundance called **Prosperity**.

Every year, the eight wealthiest nations in the world (the G8) meet for an economic summit. During one such conference considerable pressure was being brought to bear on these nations to "forgive" poorer nations their debts. Moved to speak from a different perspective, Nelson Mandela addressed the issue from his home in South Africa saying: "No more aid, we want trade."

Mandela's words point out the difference between sympathy and empathy—between *feeling sorry for someone,* and *feeling their pain or struggle.* The former gives rise to pity, which is the word used to define sympathy in the dictionary. A "sympathizer" risks getting sucked into another's suffering because "pity" itself is an emotion that works like an anesthetic, numbing us to the reality at hand and robbing us of the ability to change it. With empathy you can feel someone's sorrow instead of feeling sorry "for them," which allows you to raise the bar to compassion and causes a very different response than pity. Compassion's call to action is more likely to be one of caring or "tough love" that generates right action and a proactive intervention to lift another out of despair and defeat. The empathic response holds a higher resonance as it meets the person where they are, whereas sympathy can reinforce the stance of both the "victim" and "martyr" by standing outside and above another and showering guilt, pity, and condolences "over" their distress.

Trade, from Mandela's point of view, is the remedy that can resolve rather than simply put a band-aid over the problem of poverty. His call to action is one of proactive compassion rather than passive pity. Trade is an intervention that addresses the problem and provides a practical solution. On the other hand Aid with its beautiful intention reinforces the problem by keeping impoverished people dependant, not unlike handing a starving person a trout but withholding the secret of how to bait a hook. Trade, in Africa's case, is one of the needed "solution sets" that addresses poverty and violence.

Commerce has also been one of the most significant obstacles to war. Historically, the primary means by which both people and nations solved problems of limited resources was through taking what they needed—often by force. Neighbor attacked neighbor, tribe attacked tribe, and country attacked country. Men stole each other's resources and assets and enslaved each other's wives and children in the interest of expansion, wealth acquisition, and a conqueror's glory.

When we look at evolution as progressive stages that build on the strengths and resolve the shortcomings of what came before, we can understand the importance of the warrior stage. Cultural evolution reveals warrior consciousness as necessary for small bands and tribes to grow and develop into agrarian kingdoms. It was not until a certain level of emotional maturity started to percolate in the minds and hearts of people that the concept of peace thru negotiation and compromise become available to humanity. Commerce provided the only real antidote to war until then, and it was the carrot that led to **Peace**.

The European Union is an inspiring example of how commerce can lead to, or is an agent of, peace. Once bitter enemies who fought the bloodiest wars on any soil, European nations have united under a common market and currency and common trans-national vision. What started as a common market among six countries gave birth to the EU and the Euro. Today, with a population twice as large as the US and on a similar landmass, the EU boasts the world's largest economy. The French still love to tease the English, of course, and the English are as wry as ever when it comes to lambasting the French. And yet, when the time comes, they get down to business, because business is the common thread that makes the European Union strong and affords them an enviable quality of life. With longer than average life spans, lower crime rates, far fewer prisons, less violence in society, and a clear movement from religion to spirituality, many Europeans are already enjoying the benefits of the emerging global citizenship.

That commerce can bring former enemies together has also been demonstrated in US relations with China. When Richard Nixon went to China, ostensibly to watch the ping-pong team, he managed to strike a few business deals. At that time in history the polarization between communism and democracy had wedged an ideology gap between the US and China that was far more difficult to cross than the Pacific Ocean separating the two countries. The ping-pong strategy opened the door for these arch-enemies to become co-conspirators in the name of commerce. Trade agreements between the two countries in turn stimulated the exchange of culture; today we have an eye into China that was not possible when the Great Wall was as blinding a barrier as the Iron Curtain. Commerce was the initial bridge— or ladder as the case may be. And although China may never embrace democracy as we do, more and more people are being lifted out of poverty and China has seen greater peace than ever in its recent history.

[Sidebar] We find it fascinating to see a Harvard economist win the Nobel Prize. Dr. Muhammad Yunus is one of the first economists to sit in the company of Nelson Mandela, the Dalai Lama, Desmond Tutu, Mother Teresa and others whose work has advanced the cause of peace worldwide. Dr.Yunus was not awarded an economy prize for his work in micro-lending. He was awarded the world's most prestigious prize, the Peace prize!!

We've seen how Commerce provides a leg-up by allowing us to rise above two of the most pressing human issues: poverty and war. We've climbed up from the base of the needs pyramid in Maslow's Hierarchy where survival, safety, and community are our primary focus and concern, to the point where we are free to explore new horizons. We can now look over the ledge toward the future. While many mystics and individual seekers have experienced and fulfilled all their human needs, humanity itself is finally moving out of the primal needs of survival, security and community into a global conscious evolution. With a sufficient number of humans "coming of age" in terms of having completed the early stages of development, the possibility of humanity evolving consciously increases exponentially.

To be "Conscious" means to be "aware." Evolution is about becoming more of who we are. Conscious evolution is about being aware of whom we are becoming and being able to direct that becoming more elegantly, in the pursuit of spirituality or the divine.

In the past we evolved by adding new structures to the brain and developing new capacities in the face of survival challenges. Until now most of evolution has been unconscious—a response to pain and struggle, the tooth and claw advance of the prime directive to survive. Conscious evolution is another matter altogether; now we become active participants focused beyond mere survival to the actual advance of both our individual species and the biosphere as a whole. "Conscious evolution is the evolution of evolution, from unconscious to conscious choice. While consciousness has been evolving for billions of years, conscious evolution is new. It is part of the trajectory of human evolution, the canvas of choice before us now as we recognize that we have come to possess powers that we used to attribute to the gods." (©The Foundation for Conscious Evolution)

Barbara Marx Hubbard coined the term *conscious evolution* in the wake of the nuclear attacks on Nagasaki and Hiroshima when she recognized that humans of our generation stand on a unique and precarious precipice. According to Jean Houston, this type of precipice is something of a cultural pressure cooker that often precedes sudden leaps ahead as discussed at length in her book *Jump Time*.

Conscious evolution is unique in that it puts the pioneer in full possession of his or her ability to act with awareness and intention to bring about desired changes and engineer forward movement. The Merchant Priesthood has always been up to exactly this—the process of moving humanity along. They guided and cared for society in its infancy, providing the needs of survival, security and community by introducing agriculture, trade, democracy and the tools of commerce. By attending to the base of the Hierarchy of Needs pyramid they ushered humanity along, providing new ways to create abundance and grow in peace every step of the way.

Biological evolution is a slow process that primarily uses a process of elimination and mutation to vault ahead and move beyond limitations and shortcomings. The problems and crisis threatening our survival today are of another magnitude altogether. It is the magnitude of the threat and the depth of the dysfunction that propels us to evolve as rapidly and comprehensively as possible. The old way of fixing things through cause and effect will no longer do. We can't evolve fast enough if we are limited to the old way; our problems are simply too vast. We need, in effect, the jumpstart or power-boost that comes with the shift from unconscious to conscious in order to deal with the complexities of our current reality. In effect what we need is a capacity that only becomes available once we reach the stage of conscious evolution. That capacity, which we will simply earmark here as *miracle thinking*, will be explored in Part Three.

So what happened to the gift? Up until the current era evolution has marched humanity along for the most part unaware. For the past 2000 years that slow trudging forward has taken a chauvinistic course; Riane Eisler calls this andro-centric (male centered) paradigm "the dominator model." With the rise of chauvinism, dominion was all but lost and an authoritarian stance emerged that stripped humanity, and indeed commerce, of its sacred and feminine context, leading us to the unconscious exchange of goods and services that we experience today. What was once a sacred practice lost its soul and became brittle—men became "busy-ness-men" and women turned into "sexy-taries."

Historically, the role of the Merchant Priesthood has been to work behind the scenes, doing what they can to improve the human condition on its spiritual quest. This is their service to humanity. Their principal role and concern has always been to protect this divine Gift by creating and protecting an environment conducive to democratic principles and to encourage and keep the balance between the feminine and the masculine energies, thus enhancing the sacred in everything and keeping chauvinism at bay. They knew that democracy with its promise of equality and freedom is a prerequisite for the tools of commerce, from the coin to the stock market, not to be abused by one segment of the society at the expense of another. The gift of Sacred Commerce would rise when feminine and sacred values arose within a culture and then go underground beneath the next wave of chauvinism as the Merchant Priesthood, visionaries, and renaissance men and women formed secret societies to conceal their activities from the ruling class.

The terms *masculine* and *feminine* are used in this context not as a reference to gender differences but rather to highlight these two distinct energies and their primary modes of expression, which are in all of us regardless of gender. The difference between masculine and feminine is stated as "active" versus "passive." While the masculine is a penetrating energy that is interested in doing, acting, providing, reasoning things out, and manifesting, the feminine is a receptive energy, more concerned with being, feeling, experiencing, intuition as a means of knowing, and enjoying all that is made manifest in form. Chauvinism is defined as excessive or prejudiced loyalty to a particular gender, group or cause. Although we have moved a long way from the extreme chauvinism of the recent past, it still permeates all our senses and, if left unchecked, colors much of our life.

Fortunately, the gift of Commerce was only corrupted, not destroyed. Although it still managed to have positive impact in alleviating poverty and promoting peace, it lost its ability to help us advance spiritually. As the feminine and sacred values are coming back to the fore, in our selves and our world, humanity is reaching a level of emotional maturity where Commerce will be able to deliver on its sacred promise as never before.

The 4th Bottom Line

Trade existed from the first day humans walked the earth, but it was in Ancient Egypt that it was first instituted as a sacred practice. Since then, this sacred practice has re-emerged in many forms through every known civilization, bringing about the empowerment needed to create and evolve human societies.

Sacred Commerce is the "party-cipation" of the community in the exchange of information, goods and services that contributes to the revealing of the divine (beauty, goodness, and truth) in all and where spirituality is the bottom line.

> **[Sidebar]** Spirituality involves us in a personal relationship with God/Goddess all that is, whereas religion typically offers theology and belief as the bridge between the individual and the Divine and presupposes that the individual cannot commune with God or merge with spiritual realities on his or her own. With spirituality there are no pre-requisites, no entry rules or regulations, no judge. It is in truth a part of your life whether you are conscious of it or not. Spirituality (and for that matter all religions) view Beauty, Goodness, and Truth as at the core of all things and as a road that brings us home. The ultimate goal is for these elevated spiritual states to become permanent traits; this is what is sometimes called "enlightenment."

Sacred Commerce lifts the concept of participation to its higher octave of party-cipation—a participation sourced in celebration and joy, with choice and responsibility at its core, versus a participation that is weighted down with duty and obligation, demands or expectations. It is a participation involving co-creation, where one shares the success of that creation equally yet takes full responsibility for any failure. After all there is no one to blame.

The tradition of Sacred Commerce includes a lineage of Merchant Priests in service to humanity that appeared on every continent and throughout every period in history. Highly trained in Emotional Alchemy, they used their relationship to business as a feedback mechanism to learn and grow personally while aspiring to create prosperity for all. By meeting people's basic needs of survival, security and community, crafting a democratic environment and the tools of capitalism, they freed the individual and society to pursue their higher spiritual needs and desires that contain their unlimited potential.

In the process of manifestation or creation there are three main steps: The **Why** (the intention/purpose), the **How** (the means), and the **What** (the result or bottom line).

For hundreds of years, the concept of the bottom line in business has been synonymous with money earned, markets controlled, or power over the competition. The "*What*" has been given first order of priority at the expense of the *How* and *Why* leaving the end to justify the means and dictate the purpose. Pioneered by the human potential movement and evolved and embraced by the green and sustainable businesses, the new paradigm dethrones the absolute authority of money and measures success in broader terms. It replaces the top-down vertical patriarchal hierarchy in favor of a horizontal collaborative one.

The old business paradigm looked at the bottom line in terms of return on investment (ROI); i.e., monetary gain, profit earned. The *what*, which is to say *money*, was the primary concern. The second and third bottom lines were added by the conscious business model which became concerned with the means, the *how*, of conducting commerce. Important were matters of self-esteem, integrity, trust, character, and caring for the earth and the environment; awareness and consciousness entered the picture.

In like manner Sacred Commerce expands the concept of profit by introducing the concept and reality of *the fourth bottom line*—**Spirituality (return to Self)**—which becomes our first and primary concern. This is the return to the spiritual Self, the part of us that is in a relationship and partnership with God and in tune with the pulse of all things.

The fourth bottom line is not only the return to the spiritual Self, but also ushers in the return of the spiritual Self: You are the one you have been waiting for!

[Sidebar] During the final edit of this book, and while Googling "4th bottom line", I was delighted to find a link to Dr. Sohail Inayatullah, Professor at Tamkang University and Queensland University of Technology. He also identifies "Spirituality as the Fourth Bottom Line." In an article so titled that is posted on the metafuture.org website, Inayatullah writes: "Happiness thus becomes an inner measure of quality of life, moving away from the quantity of things. As nations move to postmodern economies, other issues are becoming more important, among them is the spiritual. It is ceasing to be associated with mediums or with feudal religions, but about life meaning... [and] the bliss beyond pleasure and pain."

In this sense, spirituality as the fourth bottom line should not be seen as selling to global corporatopia but in fact ensuring that the pendulum does not take us back to medieval times but spirals forward. This means keeping the scientific, exclusionary, mystical parts of spirituality but not acceding to the dogmatic, the sexist, the feudal dimensions. All traditions grow up in certain historical conditions. Once history changes, there is no need to keep the trappings. The message remains important but there is no need to retreat to a cave. However, the Triple Bottom Line, and spirituality as the fourth, may be a way to start to change the system so that commerce is spiritual-friendly instead of ridiculing and marginalizing it.

This spiritual return is all about the *why*. The *why* is the most important as it cuts to the chase and reveals our purpose. We no longer do business primarily for profit; we do business because it makes us more loving, intimate, caring, and happy and reveals more of who we are—our beauty, goodness, and truth. The "profit" of business becomes a greater sense of meaning in our lives and the satisfaction that comes with having impact. The pay-out of the fourth bottom line is an alignment with our destiny and a partnership with the divine. This is the *why*, and the means to this end is the *how*.

Of crucial importance to the *why* we do things is the matter of *how* we conduct ourselves; and this is where the practice of Sacred Commerce itself becomes a spiritual path. Growing awareness of our purpose allows us to turn off the auto-pilot that is conducting business, which is subconsciously fear or greed-based. We open our eyes and ears as well as our intuition and become willing to see how outdated patterns and concepts are constricting our thinking and perceiving.

With Sacred Commerce we become fierce in our dedication to build integrity, trust and character every step of the way. The means are all-important now, and they can't be sacrificed at the expense of the "*what*" or the return on investment. Actually, if placed in the sacred order of *why, how, and what*, the 'material' bottom line is achieved, and sometimes it is achieved beyond what is expected or imagined: the portal to the miraculous opens!

The fourth bottom line encourages us to first look at our motives for doing what we do. It gives us the opportunity to see through motivations such as competing with my siblings, proving to my parents that "I can amount to something," getting approval and admiration of my peers and society, or going after the "American dream" or just plain money. These programs have often unconsciously determined our choice of work.

In Sacred Commerce the *why* is given the first but not the only priority. The initial questions asked would be as simple as:

Why am I really doing this? How does it enrich my life? Does it make me a better person? Does it lift my abundance to prosperity? How does it make me more loving, more understanding, more intimate and caring? Does it make me more empathic and forgiving? Does it add to my inner peace, to my elegance and grace? How does it strengthen the quality of my relationship and partnership with God? Does it add to my joy and happiness? Does it reveal my Beauty, Goodness, and Truth?

If the activities I'm doing as my work do not lead me to such, there is little or no return to my spiritual self. There may well be a return in terms of money and that is good. There may be a return to the community and the earth, which is great. In the context of Sacred Commerce we look at the spiritual return first and then allow the unfolding of the other three bottom lines successfully with ease and elegance.

The prime directive for engaging in Sacred Commerce is this: "I am in tune with my purpose and destiny." Our choice of work is aligned with what we came here to do; our business life puts our feet squarely on that path. Each transaction, phone call, or networking event helps us on our way back home. A feeling of confidence and enthusiasm fills all that we do. The steps of getting there become the quality of being there! This spiritual bottom line is a reward no worldly success, no bank balance, no trophy, no gold medal or award can touch. This is about soul-satisfaction and the fulfillment of one's happiness.

The King of Bhutan is clearly a modern-day Merchant Priest. By pioneering the GNH "gross national happiness" concept, he provides his people an unusual yardstick to measure the nation's wealth. Instead of the traditional gross national product or GNP that measures total value of all goods and services produced, the king wants to champion his people in terms of how free, happy, and alive they are. That means equity, good governance, and harmony with nature are what this king has in mind for his people. As he guides them into the domain of democracy, his values reflect what America's founding fathers named an "inalienable right"—*the pursuit of happiness.*

Many have stumbled onto this path in the natural course of their personal or spiritual development. When Rowan and I met with the founders of Café Gratitude in San Francisco to discuss creating a chain of raw food restaurants with them, we recognized Matthew and Terces Englehardt right away. As we sat in their restaurant enjoying our meal, the atmosphere positively sparkled with gratitude; they had clearly filled the workplace with appreciation and the food with love! We shared our ideas on Sacred Commerce with our new friends, explaining that they were already doing this without the label. At one point in the conversation, I looked each of them in the eye and said, "Do you know that you are Merchant Priests?" Although I did not have a special garment or shawl to give Matthew and Terces, we were honored when they adopted the term and have come up with their own beautiful way to describe the practice: "Sacred Commerce means having 'the eternal' present in a commercial environment, making the creation of money a sacrament, and the exchange of goods and services a holy opportunity so that 'love is the bottom line'."

At no other time in history have so many felt this call of destiny and purpose. For millions of people world wide the spiritual self has been quickened and called into service and purposeful action. People stream in droves toward meaningful careers and endeavors. Sustainability, ecology, and raising consciousness in every aspect of daily life are just the beginning!

Part Two:
The Journey of the Merchant Priesthood

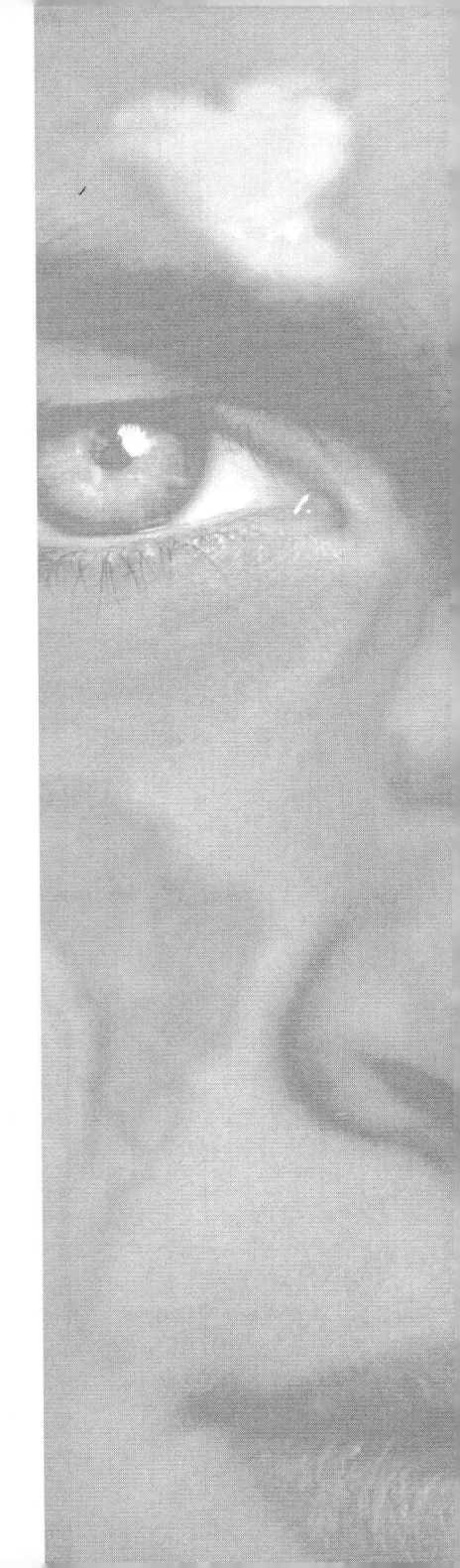

Timeline

- **2012AD**
- Benjamin Franklin (1706) — Founding of America
- The great Tulip mania (1634) — The Birth of the futures market and the seeds of the stock exchange
- **1500AD**
- The Freemasons (1200-to modern day) — Secret Societies keep the Knights mysteries alive
- Knights Templar (1118) — The keepers of the Flame, from Merchant Priests to Knights of Commerce
- **1000AD**
- Mohammad (570AD) — The Warrior of Commerce
- **500AD**
- Merlin and Arthur (480 AD) — The age of chivalry
- **0**
- **500BC**
- **1000BC**
- Moses (1200) — The baton is passed on
- Akhenaten and Nefertiti (1372) — The rise of the sacred and the feminine, the birth of the "one god"
- The reign of Thutmose the IV (1426) — The Merchant Priesthood returns
- The reign of Thutmose III (1479) — The rule of Chauvinism
- The reign of Queen Hatshepsut- (1498) — The Rise of the Merchant Priesthood
- **1500BC**

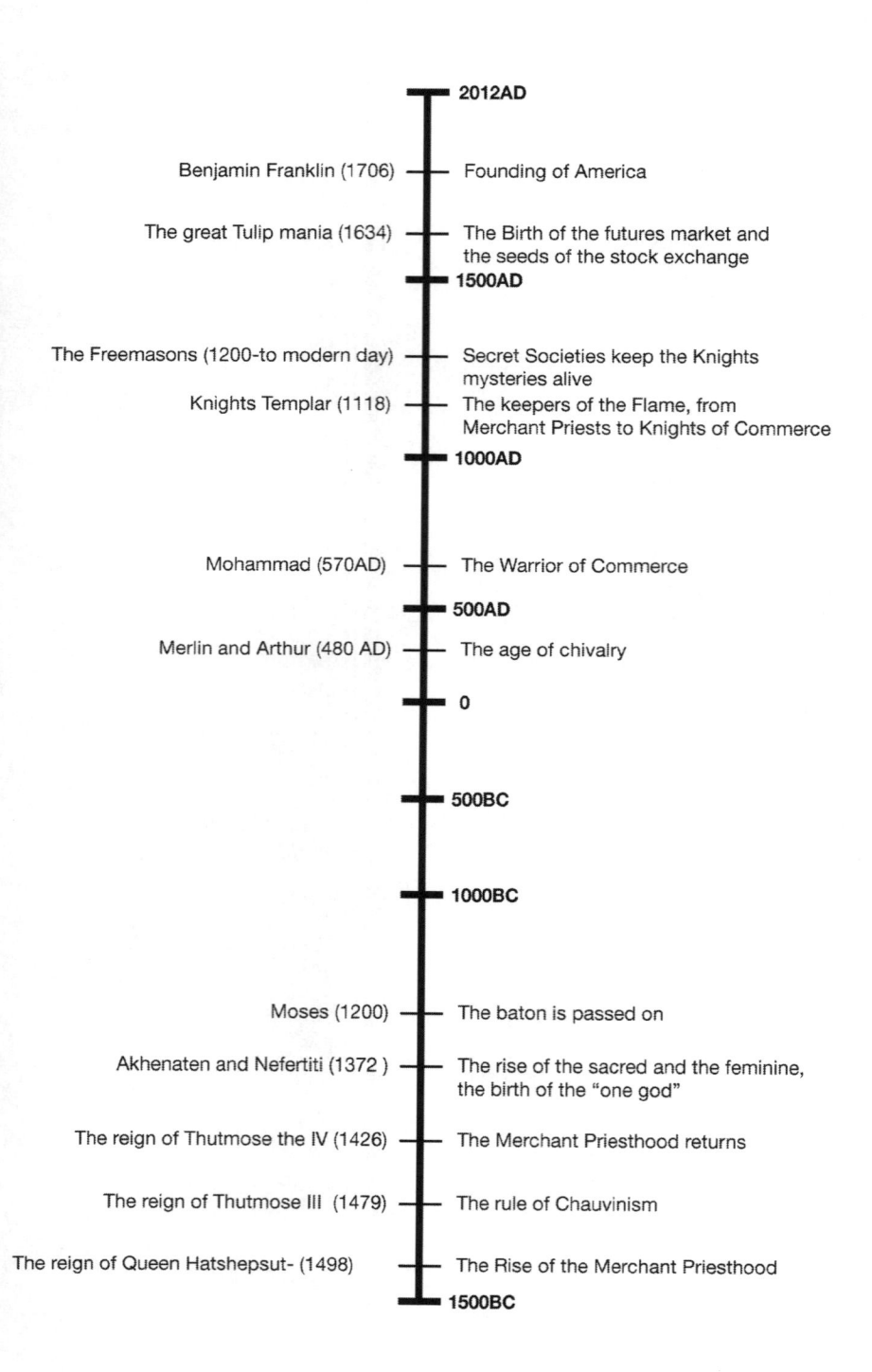

The Merchant Priesthood of the Ancient World

Long ago in ancient Egypt, the entire Mediterranean basin was dotted with temples. These shrines were more than places of worship; they served as points of power on an invisible web. The temples served as places of sanctuary for the common people. Among members of the priestly cast who had conceived and built these temples it was understood that they comprised an intricate network of nodal points. Each temple was a vortex—a node or place of joining—that drew energy from the stars and the planets. These nodes were like a lightning rod; they were designed to attracted cosmic energy and draw it toward the earth where it could be put to good use. The network of temples was perfectly aligned along specific *ley lines* that the Egyptians discerned through advanced understanding of geomancy and sacred geometry.

> [Sidebar] Geomancy, from the Greek root *geo* meaning *earth* and *manteia* or divination, is a practice of interpreting topographical markers that relies in large measure on intuitive pattern recognition. Sacred Geometry, on the other hand, is an esoteric science advanced in recent years by authors like Gregg Bradden. Gregg's research into various phenomena such as the earth's basic resonance as measured in megahertz and expressed in his theories on *zero point* have gained him a substantial audience. The notion of "ley lines" was first proposed in 1921 by Englishman Alfred Watkins when he noticed that many ancient ruins, as well as churches, hilltops, stone monuments, and castles, are often found to be positioned along straight lines. A field study to "map the

planetary grid system" conducted for Bethe Hagens, Professor of Anthropology at Governors State University, Illinois, gave us the first physical evidence (other than looking at a map) that these lines may indeed exist.

The priests who inhabited and trained in those temples lived at a very high frequency. So elevated was their personal vibration they could access spiritual insight at will and disseminate universal intelligence to the population of the region.

Each morning at sunrise, as old Sol ascended the horizon and began to kiss the sky, a wave of solar energy would move through the temples and fan out. As the radiant warmth spread across the entire country the people would awaken and rise to meet the day. With their circadian rhythms precisely attuned to the sun in this way, they awoke profoundly revitalized and refreshed.

The priests of ancient Egypt had vocations and roles above and beyond what we are accustomed to in our time. Some Egyptian priests never left the temple; they served by staying in perpetual dialogue with the universal current of life. Other priests were scribes, healers, teachers, mediators, and celebrants. Still others were known as Merchant Priests. Certain members of the priesthood took up Sacred Commerce as a mission to serve humanity.

Whereas Healing Priests worked with people on an individual basis, the Merchant Priesthood focused on society as a whole. They attended to the bigger picture and worked to balance the collective psychic state.

The Merchant Priests traveled specific energy pathways that were known to them because of their high vibration. These energy pathways, or ley lines, became the trade routes that led from one temple to the next, allowing precious goods to be exchanged between regions. Turquoise, for example, would be exchanged for herbs or incense and fine fabrics would be exchanged for hand-woven baskets. Items of exchange were primarily those high vibration prized objects and elements that raised people's consciousness, and whose presence made you feel more elated, either by their beauty or by their intrinsic resonance/vibration, like the healing vibration of precious essential oils from flowers.

Whether animal, mineral, or plant, the value of the goods lay in the fact that they were infused with spiritual power and because the item carried the frequencies that helped maintain the balance of energy in a particular place. This was a work of extraordinary refinement. Only much later as culture began to slide into darker times did trade devolve into the unconscious exchange of goods and services that we experience in many segments of the marketplace today.

Merchant Priests knew that a healthy society must have a solid foundation. Principles of flow, balance, and abundance were understood as essential, and commerce was a key means to that end. The Merchant Priesthood assumed responsibility for assuring abundance and allowing goods to flow freely throughout the realm to the entire population. They watched over and shepherded the ebb and flow of exchange between the different levels of society, thus ensuring the wealth did not get bottlenecked. No one place or social class could pool resources at the expense of another.

Goods were viewed as vessels of energy. They were also a means to engage and connect on a personal level. Trade, in many ways, functioned as social intercourse. Great value was placed on cultivating empathy and friendly relationships; these formed the basis of commercial dealings. These qualities and a general sense of conviviality fostered a balanced psychic state in individuals. Relationships were understood to be the means by which a harmonious psychic state is established throughout a culture. In sum, the Merchant Priests knew that Emotional Intelligence was a prerequisite for prosperity. After all, it was prosperity rather than profit that was most important to them.

Training in the Merchant Priesthood involved many, many years of building knowledge and understanding which they infused into their commercial dealings. Often, though not always, these priests were recognized and chosen for the calling in their infancy. Senior priests would tour the villages looking for children who showed signs of having been part of the Merchant Priesthood in a previous life. This is not unlike the practice in Tibet wherein lamas look for an honored teacher to return in his next incarnation.

An Egyptian priest would approach a candidate and listen to his heartbeat. Then, beating a drum in that rhythm, he would watch to see if the child moved in a certain way. If the child showed physical integration and made full use of his lower body, that meant he was a likely candidate. Other tests would follow, similar again to those used by the Tibetans. For example, a number of objects would be placed in the child's view, among them an object typically carried by a Merchant Priest. If the child recognized and reached for that object, it was taken as a sign. Or a leopard skin—one of the symbols of the priesthood—would be placed on the ground among many other skins. If the child crawled over and sat on the leopard skin, this was another good indication he/she had been a Merchant Priest in a former life.

This practice was also common among the Hopi. When children of the tribe reached two years old, a collection of toys would be presented to them. The tribal elders would watch to see what toy became the child's favorite. The child who favored a drum or a rattle, the tools of the shaman, would be given to a different teacher than the child who consistently played with the bow and arrow or other tools of a warrior.

In some cases a specific body type—a short, dwarf-like stocky frame—was the clue that an individual was destined for the Merchant Priesthood. Given that the Merchant Priests watched over the temple treasuries, some of the priests had to be small enough to pass through the secret entrance where the riches were stored. The deity that presided over and protected the Merchant Priesthood was the god Bes. A dwarf himself, Bes also presided over birth—the gate between the spiritual and material world. The first to represent success in the form of the portly gentleman, his fullness also represented his alliance with midwives and his capacity to bring forth a soul to the earth plane. For Egyptians, to greet an incoming soul with the means by which s/he could satisfy all material needs was essential—an ethical imperative that society took upon itself. From their perspective humans were spiritual beings coming to earth to experiment on the physical plane and were to be provisioned properly. Like the laughing Buddha, Bes was the god of laughter and joy and is often represented with his tongue sticking out. His earthy joy was transformative; through laughter he transmuted the negative energies of fear, anger, and jealousy into their higher frequencies of compassion, passion and empathy.

Initiation and Training

Emotional Intelligence was the primary focus of Merchant Priesthood training. This involved a deep education that spanned years if not decades and led to a profound understanding of the lower centers and the root emotions associated with each. Once initiated on the path, the Merchant Priest-in-training began to explore and develop the "hara"—the vital center below the naval that is the seat of emotional power. Both men and women took up this training.

Priests and priestesses alike were called to the Merchant Priesthood path, and the training for each was first and foremost this study and mastery of the emotional realm. While both genders trained rigorously and engaged in similar activities, the male priests where more engaged in trading activities and traveled extensively, while the priestesses were more responsible for maintaining a high vibration or resonance. She did this by entering a meditative state and expanding her awareness to a point where she was literally responsible for crafting the collective emotional sphere of a gathering or a temple. She first became very still inside and then called in specific resonances, drawing forward the eternal verities of beauty, goodness, and truth. For the female Merchant Priest this form of meditation was a process of both inner and outer refinement.

As part of this early training the acolyte—often a child—was brought to market so that s/he could witness and grow accustomed to the intense, ever-shifting emotional environment surrounding trade negotiations. They learned to recognize and "read" emotions in fine detail, attending to many layers and levels of expression. From physical manifestations such as facial expression, muscle tension, skin tone, vocal quality, and even heart rate and blood pressure the Merchant Priest learned to sense the texture and temperature of the emotional side of trade. This would—in time—give the Merchant Priest the ability to equalize and balance the energy of emotions that swirled around the marketplace.

Imagine for a moment a Zen master walking around the Stock Market in the heat of a trading day while brokers and traders clamor all around. This is the depth of presence and awareness the Merchant Priests carried with them when they walked through the markets. The Merchant Priest knew how to shift the clamoring into a higher order of exchange.

This, then, was the Merchant Priests' ministry: Raising the frequency/vibration of an emotion whereby the emotion is "lifted/raised" from a lower octave to a higher one, such as in lifting fear to a level where it could be felt as *concern*. Fear tends to freeze a human being, whereas concern arouses compassion which in turn leads to action. Likewise, a Merchant Priest could also transform anger into courage, and courage into passion and so on.

Humanity had very little emotional maturity at the time when the Merchant Priesthood was most active. In fact, the general public was largely illiterate when it came to emotions. The marketplace was rife with envy, jealousy, anger, and even outright rage. The Merchant Priest would literally "minister" to the collective psychic state. He would go to the market, sit in the corner and close his eyes in meditation. With his vast capacity for empathy, he would suck in all the emotions, taking into his own body all the swirling fear, anger and jealousy. Then, using his body and mind as an alchemical chamber, he would add a drop of joy to these raw emotions and transform them into compassion, passion, and empathy (this will be fully explained in the chapter on Emotional Alchemy). Then he would breathe these refined emotional frequencies back out into the market place, infusing the shared psychic space with higher, more balanced emotional tone.

Moreover, a Merchant Priest was trained to recognize and contain jealousy. Jealousy is called the green monster for good reason and along with anger and fear is one of the most troublesome of human emotions because of the passion it evokes in the being. Merchant Priests were highly sensitized to jealousy, learning first to experience it fully in themselves. Tending to emotion in a literate and intelligent way, the acolyte learned to *listen* to what the green monster had to say. By respecting the emotion as a communication containing vital information, he would listen to its signal and learn.

The more they were able to contain their own life energies in this way, the more they were able to feel the emotions of others and manage the collective psychic state for the greater good, without anyone even knowing they were doing it. With training the Merchant Priests became masters of this process. In a sense they were the first real diplomats; theirs was the work of negotiation. Humanity had so little emotional maturity that it needed the intervention of the Merchant Priesthood to minister to the emotional sphere of the society. Not until a level of emotional maturity began to percolate in people's minds and hearts did the concept of negotiation become accessible. Until that time it was the Merchant Priest's job. They could literally assist and, in a sense, "sculpt" the emotional reality of the marketplace. Some were so skilled they would simply resonate with the higher aspect of a particular emotion and radiate it outward to counteract base feelings before they took hold. This was the Merchant Priests' unique science.

Managing the lower centers in this way was not limited to the sphere of business. The Merchant Priests also stayed in touch with and maintained balance in the general psychic tone of the culture and were responsible for more practical things like reading the Nilometer—a device that monitored the rise and fall of the Nile River.

The Egyptians had a harmonious relationship with the Nile, thanks to the work of the Merchant Priests. The great river was essential to their livelihood and to the growth of agriculture. In addition, it was a primary line of communication—the lifeline that fed travel, transportation, and trade—as essential as satellites are to us today. The Nilometer warned when floods were coming and helped foresee whether they would be high or low, early or late. With a deep appreciation for the forces of nature and astronomy, the Merchant Priests understood that the floods made the land fertile and added to the overall abundance.

Upon reading the Nilometer the priests would issue instructions on the ideal time to plant and indeed what to plant. If an irregular flood pattern interrupted a planting season, the priests could sense and stabilize the fear and anxiety that moved through the collective.

The priests were also trained to read psychic changes that occurred with cycles of the moon. Lunar influences on both individuals and the collective were noted and addressed. Perhaps the most highly evolved—in terms of psychic development—that we have seen in human history, the Egyptians were also deeply embodied and grounded in the practical world. It was this balance between the emphasis and value placed on psychic sensitivity and the grounded practical abilities that allowed the Merchant Priests to become one of the most respected of the priestly castes.

Their sensitivity to the subtleties of psychic irregularities is why the leopard became their symbol. Like the sleek cat whose night-time stealth is legendary, Merchant Priests could see into the dark of the human subconscious. They were masters at reading both individual people and the collective psyche. In today's world this ability has been reduced to certain groups of mediums and psychics or degraded and placed in the hands of tabloids. In Egypt the priests—not the paparazzi—oversaw the dark side. They could sense negative energies the moment they began to emerge and transmute them before external damage occurred.

The Egyptians understood that a healthy society relied on the unique contribution of every part. The Healer Priests, for example, had an extraordinary degree of compassion. This earned them deep love and respect not only from the general public but also from the other priestly castes. Although Merchant Priests were also trained to develop compassion, the Healer Priests were the ones who fully mastered that quality.

Plato divided ancient Egyptian society into three parts. The Craftsmen represented the digestive forces; they digested the food of the gods—the raw material of the earth, which, in turn, became art (beauty). The Soldiers represented both the heart and the mastery of the three emotions that reside within the heart—love, joy, and sorrow. The greatest soldiers were those who had been baptized by love, because they had something to fight for that was true (goodness). Before going to battle, soldiers would seek the blessing of the lion god Sekhmet. Their hearts would thus be cleansed of all conflict, allowing them to concentrate and focus the mind with single-pointed purpose on the matter at hand. Finally, the Philosophers and thé scribes represented the head (truth). These three parts worked together as a seamless, organic whole.

Comparatively speaking, the Merchant Priesthood was like a post-doctorate-level training. Its members were tested and trained and conducted deep personal research into the psychic and practical functioning of all three levels of society. These men expressed their love as concern for the big picture, rather than personal love. They were concerned for the overall welfare of their people and kept a keen eye on the whole. Functionally, their main job was like that of Plato's Craftsmen. At the same time, they infused all commercial undertakings with genuine empathy. The empathic and intuitive sensitivity brought to bear was both lubricant and shock-absorber, allowing everything to flow and run smoothly.

Origins, Legend, and Myth

Legend tells that the Merchant Priesthood thrived—and may well have been birthed—in the now mythical land known as Atlantis. When that civilization disappeared beneath the waves, a few survivors escaped and remnants of its culture surfaced in Egypt and many other parts of the world.

Historically we see the first real signs of a Merchant Priesthood during Queen Hatshepsut's reign from 1479 to 1457 BC. Known as the era of the "New Kingdom," this period saw Egypt develop into a great empire as wealth and new ideas spread across the country. By the time Queen Hatshepsut began her reign, officials were already being selected on merit instead of the more traditional system, which passed authority through family lines and inheritance. This strongly suggests the influence of the Merchant Priesthood, who—by their nature and the nature of their work—was predisposed to democratic principles.

Scenes painted on the walls of Hatshepsut's funerary temple depict various trade guilds bringing offerings to the queen. These guilds are another indication of the presence of the Merchant Priesthood. Queen Hatshepsut encouraged and supported their role among the priestly caste, raising them to the highest office and esteem during her reign. At her bequest the Merchant Priests opened the trade routes to encourage commerce with other cultures. The route between Egypt and the Land of Punt, which is located near present day Somalia, was opened during this time. The Merchant Priests served the benevolent queen well, and this new trade route allowed her subjects to enjoy highly prized imports—ivory, spices, gold, and aromatic plants. Simultaneously these activities began to bring different cultures and communities together to learn from each other.

Unlike statues or murals depicting other Egyptian pharaohs, paintings of Hatshepsut show the Merchant Priests standing tall rather than bowing in the presence of their Queen. This shows strongly the esteem she had for them and suggests the democratic principle of equality was valued during her reign.

> [Sidebar] In June of 2007, while we were finalizing this manuscript we were pleasantly surprised, and consider it a good omen, to hear that Zahi Hawass, Egypt's chief archaeologist, held a news conference in Cairo to announce that scientists had identified the mummy of Queen Hatshepsut. Although the mummy in question was found in 1903 at a site believed to be the tomb of the Queen's attendant, a century would pass before the clue to the mummy's identity—a tooth—was matched up with the remains. It was common practice for Egyptian embalmers to set aside teeth and then place them in a box bearing their owner's name. A wooden box containing a molar tooth and inscribed with the queen's name was found in 1881 in a cache of royal mummies hidden away at Deir al-Bahari temple a thousand meters away from the tomb. A perfect match between tooth and jaw is apparently as reliable as a fingerprint for identification purposes.

Hatshepsut's successor, Thutmosis III, undid nearly all the progress his step-mother had made during her twenty-year rule. Favoring war over trade, Thutmosis displaced the Merchant Priests and stripped them of almost all their authority so they were no longer influential. This is typical of the history of the Merchant Priesthood: it would rise when feminine and sacred values arose within a culture and then go underground beneath the next wave of chauvinism, forming secret societies to conceal their activities from the ruling class. The Merchant Priests were esteemed during Hatshepsut's reign, and the people enjoyed abundance as a result. When the Merchant Priests were demoted, the delicate social and psychic balance began to wobble. This opened the way for Thutmosis III to make war against former trade partners. Instead of trading goods and sharing culture, he began to vanquish and conquer.

A war economy tends to give the temporary illusion of wealth and, indeed, Egypt seemed to prosper under Thutmosis III. Yet he nearly bankrupted the country. The remnants of the Merchant Priesthood managed to stave off complete economic collapse by conspiring to support the next pharaoh, Thutmosis IV.

The new pharaoh knew that the Giza complex had always been the core energy source of Egypt. In a vision, he saw that if the complex could once again be sparked into life, it had the power to re-stabilize and energize the entire country. He went on to rebuild the country's infrastructure. In so doing, he reinstated many of the displaced Merchant Priests. During his reign, Egypt once again prospered.

[Sidebar] Known in modern times as one of the 7 Wonders of the World, the pyramids at Giza are the most majestic necropolis (cemetery) known. The complex is comprised of The Great Pyramid, the smaller Pyramid of Khafre, the smaller still Pyramid of Menkaure, a number of satellite "queens" pyramids, causeways and valley pyramids, as well as the stunning Great Sphinx. Legend tells of the Merchant Priesthood designing an initiatory encounter for Thutmosis IV involving the Sphinx. The site had been barred during the previous pharaoh's reign because it had been such a powerful vortex for initiations. When Thutmosis IV came into power, the Merchant Priests managed to gain access and arranged for the new ruler to sleep between the Sphinx's paws. A kind of giant cosmic tuning fork, the paws create a high frequency energy field. While sleeping in this most sacred of sacred spots, the pharaoh had a revelation followed by vision after vision of various civil projects that would revitalize the Giza complex and the Sphinx itself. These civil projects in turn revived an economy that had become depleted and crippled by years of war.

With the reign of Akhenaten, the reach and influence of the Merchant Priests once again expanded. They were given responsibility for myriad construction projects from temple restoration to the building of an entirely new capital city.

Akhenaten was a great champion and leader of the Merchant Priesthood, and a revolutionary in many ways. Some of the most essential features of the Merchant Priesthood's vision of a healthy society were ushered to the fore during Akhenaten's reign. People openly worshiped Ra as the One God, a practice that had formerly been limited to a hidden mystery cult. Although it was his father, Amenophis III, who had initiated the movement toward monotheism—going so far as to proclaim his young son "the Messiah"—it was really Akhenaten who spearheaded monotheism by bringing worship of Ra out into the open.

In the course of advancing this new form of religion, he liberated Egyptian art from rigidly stylized forms. Statues of Akhenaten and his wife, Queen Nefertiti, look strangely modern. As works of art, they almost appear to be cousins of much later works by Modigliani and Rodin. He also allowed the Merchant Priests to bring artists from Crete to Egypt. Minoan art introduced a different style and a new way of looking at the world that was less encumbered by an exaggerated belief that all rewards lay in the afterlife. At that point in Cretan history civilization centered around celebration and investing oneself in the joys of "here and now." The life of the senses was highly valued, not as hedonistic indulgence, but as a soulful celebration of the spirit in matter. Throughout their entire history, the sacred purpose and mission of the Merchant Priesthood has been to unite spirit and matter.

Akhenaten fostered the vision of a non-violent, almost democratic society, and his reign saw the first flowering of a rational philosophy as well as the bare beginnings of a school of scientific thought. Akhenaten even dreamed of a single civilization throughout the Mediterranean, united by a complex web of trade routes and free trade among all peoples—one of the first seeds of what we now talk of as the Globalization movement.

Akhenaten was a revolutionary in another sense as well; some consider him to have foreshadowed feminism. He took his wife as an equal and ruled side by side with her rather than with her "at his side" as other sovereigns of the time. In essence, Akhenaten brought the feminine back and opened the door to the everyday sacred. Oddly enough, this was also his Achilles heel. Akhenaten and Nefertiti were both so focused—some say, obsessed—with steering Egypt back onto a spiritual track that they tended to ignore certain threats. Hostile neighbors, intent on military invasion and intrigues against the pharaoh by the priests of Thebes, began to loom large. These negative energies grew in force. Meanwhile, the pharaoh and his wife existed at such a high vibration they could barely keep themselves in their bodies. The art they left behind has led some to surmise that they went so far in their process of merging spirit and matter that matter itself nearly de-materialized.

Akhenaten was the last pharaoh to revere Joseph, the Hebrew with the many-colored coat. An early Merchant Priest,

Joseph had lived in Egypt hundreds of years before Akhenaten. You may recall the story of Joseph being sold into slavery in Egypt by his brothers after he told them of his dream. In the dream Joseph saw a sheaf of corn standing upright in a circle of eleven sheaves. All the other sheaves were bowing to the one in the middle; the honored sheaf was Joseph. This exacerbated the fact that Jacob, the father of all twelve brothers, had always favored Joseph who was his youngest. The dream image got the better of the brothers and they secretly sold their baby brother into slavery.

Once in Egypt, Joseph did not remain a slave for long. Word of him as a gifted interpreter of dreams reached the present pharaoh who'd had a troubling series of dreams his advisors could not help him understand. Joseph was called in to discuss the dream. The Pharaoh had dreamt of seven fat cows, then of seven lean cows that ate the fat ones. The Egyptian priests had not been able to interpret the symbolism in cattle with protruding ribs.

Joseph interpreted the dream, saying it was prophetic. He indicated that the cows were symbolic and predicted seven prosperous years that would be followed by seven lean ones characterized by famine and drought. Joseph recommended the pharaoh make wise use of resources that had been saved from previous years of plenty and store them in granaries—sustainability in its earliest form. The pharaoh took his advice, commissioned Joseph to build the granaries and, sure enough, the famine came. During the lean years Egypt was the only country in the whole region with grain—the measure and standard of wealth at that time. The pharaoh rewarded Joseph by promoting him to a position of leadership as the head of the Merchant Priesthood. In ancient Egyptian, the word Joseph came to mean "head of the granaries."

Visions played yet another role in Joseph's ascent to high office as the greatest Merchant Priest of his time. He championed the use of the Nilometer. With it he was able to foresee whether the Nile flood would be high or low and could advise the people on what to plant and where. While other agrarian societies in the region suffered, Egypt faired well. During the seven long years of famine, Joseph's father and brothers came to Egypt in search of grain. They approached the Master of the Granaries on bended knee and begged for food. Joseph's dream about the sheaves of corn had been prophetic after all. He didn't reveal his identity right away, but gave his family all they needed. He showed stern compassion as well as generosity.

Among the many hidden morals in this tale is an important layer of meaning that can help us understand the influence of the Merchant Priests. As we have seen, the Merchant Priests always stood for the democratic process. In the ascent of the youngest brother, the story questions the traditional social hierarchy. The story shows us that life has its own intelligent process and will gather whatever forces are needed to manifest its inherent patterns. Those patterns are seeds or archetypes that have been there from the beginning. One such pattern is the tendency of organisms to move toward an egalitarian system of flow—flow of energy in all its different forms and directions. That is what we really mean by democracy—a system that allows optimum flow rather than a stop-gap hierarchy that keeps energy locked up in privileged compartments. The social system at the time of Joseph sought to uphold patriarchal authority by passing it down through the eldest male.

As the story goes, Jacob and his sons stayed in Egypt. Over time the Hebrews became an honored people there. Many Hebrews were trained in the Merchant Priesthood. Their contribution and involvement in commerce can be traced to that time.

By the time Akhenaten took the throne many years later,

conflict between the Hebrews and Egyptians had begun to stir. His reign was peppered with conflict from the start, largely because of his allegiance and loyalty to his mother, Queen Tiye, who was Hebrew. High priests in Thebes, the capital city, objected to god Ra being raised above all others because this reduced their power as clergy for the polytheistic religion.

The tension became so great that Akhenaten had to leave Thebes and travel north along the Nile. There, on virgin ground, he built a new capital. In the end, he and Nefertiti disappeared in the face of assassination threats. The Theban priests who conceived the plan to assassinate Akhenaten devised a plan to take possession of his corpse. Legend says they intended to use their magic arts to tap into Akhenaten's memory banks and distort the esoteric knowledge pertaining to the One God he had received from his father. Akhenaten's disappearance foiled their plan. Rumor has it the two dematerialized, transmuting themselves into pure light—but one day we may yet find their mummies.

Before Akhenaten disappeared he initiated one of his advisors in the northern city into the full mysteries of monotheistic religion. Like the pharaoh's mother, that advisor was a Hebrew—the man we know as Moses. In addition to introduceing him to the notion of One God, Akhenaten shared the secrets of the Merchant Priesthood with Moses. We muse that the secret scrolls associated with the Ark of the Covenant may well have contained a master plan for a balanced society that had at its core the practice of Sacred Commerce and Emotional Alchemy. Likely Moses passed the esoteric knowledge down through other highly placed Hebrews while handing over to the people a set of simple behavioral guidelines known as the Ten Commandments.

Following Akhenaten's disappearance, the Theban priests led Egypt back to polytheism, obliterating every trace of Akhenaten's name. But the seed of a monotheistic vision, as well as the seeds of the Merchant Priesthood, had been planted. Among the Hebrews it silently began to grow. This is how Moses during the reign of Akhenaten's successor, Rameses, came to embody the knowledge and vision of Akhenaten as both a High Priest of the prevailing Egyptian rites and an advisor in the northern city.

The reason Moses led the Hebrews out of Egypt was to free them from slavery. Rameses was unable to contain his jealousy, and felt the Hebrews had become too prosperous. Their growing numbers and wealth made him nervous, so he enslaved the entire people. Previously, Egypt was a multi-cultural society; many different ethnic groups flourished and moved freely across its unguarded borders. Rameses stopped the flow of free trade and tried to centralize power, holding it exclusively for himself and his chosen priests. The Merchant Priests were sent to remote regions of the country where their influence would be minimal; those who were of Hebrew descent were enslaved.

Moses, highly skilled in the art of empathy and Emotional Alchemy was able to unleash the plagues on Egypt by redirecting Rameses' personal emotions and projecting them back on to the collective (in ancient Egypt the Pharaoh *was* Egypt); in this case—to use the language of the Bible—"the Pharaoh's heart was unusually hard." Finally, Rameses was forced to let the Hebrew people go on their way.

> [Sidebar] The point of this history is to provide a context for where we are today. What we see and who we are now is built on myriad societies that came before, honed by the process of evolution. History is one long journey of refinement, and we are the ones—both as individuals and as a collective—who continue to be refined. The task at hand, and what we believe is evolution's trajectory, is the harmonious co-existence of all humans with the earth.

The long-awaited Promised Land enticed Moses into the wilderness with his people. He took the secrets with him and initiated the rabbis into monotheism and the principles of Merchant Priesthood. While in the desert, he gave his followers the gift of writing and the law—the Ten Commandments. The Hebrew people were thus endowed with both the means and structure for a whole new stage of growth and development.

Eventually, his descendant, Solomon, built a temple in Jerusalem, much of it financed by the gold the Hebrews had carried out of Egypt. Solomon, with his principles of fairness and justice for all and not just the privileged, was the true inheritor of Moses and the Merchant Priesthood lineage. It was he who conducted the sacred rites that activated the Ark of the Covenant.

> [Sidebar] When I discussed this with Dr Gabriel Cousins, a dear friend and teacher of Kabbalah, he told me that these sacred rites [activating the resonance of the ark to create an energy field conducive to the work at hand] featured ten rabbis on one side and ten princes (one of the names given a high merchant) on the other.

From the land of the Israelites the Merchant Priesthood continued to spread across the eastern Mediterranean into Greece where they were instrumental in the founding of many great city-states, among them Thebes, named after Akhenaten's capital in Egypt.

Several hundred years later, when Alexander invaded Egypt, the Greeks built a completely new capital city on the very site where Akhenaten's had stood.

The Greeks named their new city Hermopolis (which later was renamed Alexandria) in honor of the god Hermes. Hermes was the messenger god, the god of commerce and writing, and the god of all forms of exchange, equivalent to the god Bes in Egypt. Remember as well that Moses, God's messenger to the Hebrews, was the one who gave them writing.

What we are suggesting is that it is possible to trace an unbroken line of senior Merchant Priests at least from Queen Hatshepsut down through Moses to Oedipus and the founding of the cradles of democracy in the city-states of Greece.

The Merchant Priesthood, through its Greek influence, was instrumental in the founding of the European world. This included introducing the concept of democracy and influence on the creation of the first coins. First introduced in Lydia, a seafaring neighboring state of the Greeks, around 700 BC, the new coins replaced metal rings that had been used by the Egyptians as rudimentary coinage. It was not until the Greek civilization emerged that coinage became a full-fledged instrument of trade and exchange. A great dream that originated with Akhenaten, the invention of coin vastly facilitated trade and interaction between all the peoples of the Mediterranean.

The work of the Merchant Priests was not limited to the Middle East, however. In the Far East a related set of underlying "Merchant Priest" values also began to spread. Let us consider Lao Tse, for example. The great sage of Chinese Taoism introduced the notion of "inner ecology." Also called Feng Shui, this extensive and detailed practice involved the relationship between emotional life and geomantic energy flows. Because of Lao Tse's Taoist influence, Chinese cities were organized in such a way as to facilitate the harmonization of the emotional life of the populace. Monks held and fulfilled responsibilities much like those assumed by the Merchant Priests in Egypt. Lao Tse essentially united the urban social structures with the larger overall ecology. Later, of course, China became corrupt, until eventually the Mongols moved in and revitalized the culture with *their* passion.

> [Sidebar] A little known fact is that the Egyptians practiced a kind of emotional Feng Shui similar to our modern Feng Shui where each area of the house is represented as a part of the bagua (the Feng Shui blueprint). In today's Feng Shui bagua each section is made up of the key elements of our lives, such as our "abundance" and "relationships." In Egypt these areas were more related to emotions.

In Lao Tse's time, some two and a half thousand years ago, the flow of ideas and goods was unimpeded due to the harmonious emotional state of the country. The culture was deeply aligned with the natural energy flows of the earth and these, of course, became the trade routes, later know as the famous "Silk Road." Fifteen hundred years after Lao Tse's time, the Chinese Merchant Priests invented paper money; it was they who passed the knowledge of the earliest type of printing press on to Marco Polo.

By exciting the authorities into printing paper money, these commerce adventurers (priests) were able to introduce the printing press in Europe. With this development and the spread of literacy that ensued, the monopoly on knowledge was broken and no longer was education the exclusive privilege of the elite. This continued the process of leveling the playing field, lifting another roadblock towards democracy.

The Merlin and Arthur Legacy
To Europe and the King's Court

The concern for attunement with nature evidenced among the Chinese and Egyptians also lies at the heart of the tales of King Arthur. It can even be argued that Arthur and Merlin were the greatest Merchant Priests during that time of intense activity on the part of the Merchant Priesthood.

Legend tells of Merlin's tutelage under Saint Kevin of Ireland. During the Dark Ages Saint Kevin did all he could to keep breathing life into a dying civilization. With Europe in chaos after the fall of the Roman Empire, the Celtic Christians in Ireland were the continent's lifeline to civilization and the sole store of knowledge. Many Merchant Priests were born among the Irish at that time. When the Romans left following a series of failed harvests and a variety of events on the continent the Merchant Priests began their work in earnest. Their first task was to restore the use of lunar and solar calendars knowing this knowledge could help steer the population in the right direction—toward a life in harmony with the planetary cycles and energy flows. With the help of the calendars, the knowledge of what to plant, of when and where to plant, and of how to avert famine was restored.

It is interesting to note that the Arthurian legend is an odd mix of time frames and metaphors that lead into and from the tale of Camelot. The historical figure King Arthur reigned during the 5th century, but the Arthurian legend emerged hundreds of years after the fact. The saga of the Round Table and the Holy Grail started with Arthur and Merlin but were embellished by and mixed with tales of chivalry and knights for hundreds of years after the fact.

It is important to see that legends are allegories that reveal the workings of the human mind and of a man's relationship to the community. For this reason tales like Camelot carry deep truths that need to be deciphered for their full impact to reach us and deliver an essential understanding of human nature. Stories and parables have been used throughout time by the priestly castes for just this purpose—the dissemination of knowledge. Myths are a transmission of archetypal energy and soul wisdom, designed to nourish the spirit and help us grow in an ethical direction. In light of this the question becomes: How do we best interpret the Arthurian legends with respect to the Merchant Priests' ideology? This question has fascinated me for quite some time. My work with Emotional Intelligence and the stories of Merlin and Arthur told to me by my friend Lazaris pointed the way to the answer.

Each knight at the Round Table not only represented a different family and hierarchy, he represented a *specific temperament*. Accordingly, each was perceived as being suited to a particular task, which he was thereupon assigned. At the same time, each knight was given an equal place at the Round Table; we know that the Merchant Priests held the principle of equality as paramount. This did not mean, however, that everything or everyone must be the same—a logical, but counter-intuitive interpretation. True equality does not imply a level playing field where all things are equal so much as a discerning playing field where all things have their proper place in relation to the whole of culture and history

What the Merchant Priesthood championed was a view of the whole that recognized the unique value of each and every member of society, from the most humble to the highest. Each person of every class was to be accorded due respect and an appropriate share of the overall prosperity of the culture.

By extension the Merchant Priests saw every emotion as having its rightful place within the overall ecology of both the individual and society as a whole. Metaphorically the Round Table and the diverse characters who sat around it were a complete map of the psychic states necessary for the proper functioning of the Kingdom. Symbolically, the "kingdom" can be interpreted as either society or an individual.

The urban court and, indeed, all individuals were likewise viewed from this frame. When every knight fulfilled his *particular* duty, a *general* integration across all the emotions was the result and, therefore, peace reigned in the kingdom. Under these conditions of integration all could enjoy the natural flow of knowledge and resources between the different segments of society and across other cultures. This was the map represented by Camelot. As a symbol of the "New Jerusalem," Camelot is that city where heaven comes to earth and the beauty of the natural order is replicated in human society.

A number of esoteric and mystical teachings point out that the knights also represent the potential for the natural order to be replicated in a single human being. This teaching sees the Knights as symbolic of personality types that also correspond to the signs on the zodiac. My favorite interpretation is the map of chivalry offered by our friend Lazaris. This view sees each knight as the embodiment of a specific quality. These qualities are honor, loyalty, nobility, virtue, grace, trust, courage, courtesy, gallantry, authority, service, and humility. When all twelve quailties exist within a being, their frequencies combine and coalesce. The synergy of the twelve (chivalry) is vastly greater than the sum of the parts. Seen from this perspective, the Knights of the Round Table are an invitation to embody the full spectrum of our humanity in its most noble form. The role of the feminine in this development is paramount, thus the designation of women as the "Ladies of the Round." They were not necessarily the knights' wives or lovers. They could be a friend, sister, crone, wife or female counterpart. The Ladies of the Round learned to attune themselves to the subtle frequencies of their knight's unique quality of courage, trust, gallantry, etc. Their role was as important as that of the knights. It is the woman who triggers and inspires chivalry in a man. Their job was to hold the space and, thereby, tap into what today's scientists call *resonance* or *field effect*.

Where does the Grail come in? Legend finds the Knights of the Round Table searching after the mystical vessel—a cup or urn in which the blood of a crucified Christ had supposedly been caught. But the Grail never really belonged to this dimension of reality. Rather, it was a supreme symbol of the spiritualization of matter. In essence, the Grail represents the healing of the Immaculate Heart; that is to say, the heart of Christ and the heart of the whole Christian story.

The Knights of the Round Table could only become truly united by the acquisition of the Grail. In other words, men can only become truly united in the radiance of love. Love is the deepest essence of our emotional being; it rules all the other emotions. At heart, love was the whole purpose of the quest, symbolized by the vision of the Holy Grail. Wherever the Grail appeared—and credible appearances occurred in extremely diverse locations—it sparked intense desire on the part of those who sought it. Merlin was given his first vision of the true meaning of the Holy Grail when he was with his mentor St. Kevin in Ireland. But reports of the Grail being seen in many other places across both Britain and on the continent were common. Various churches laid claim to having the chalice at different times, and none of them were proved fraudulent. But the Grail was a most challenging quest. The inability to acquire it made it all the more venerated and ever more inspiring to its seekers. Accordingly, the Grail generated huge flows of pilgrims across Europe, which of course meant a renewed flow of ideas, knowledge, and commerce.

This marked the beginning of what we now know as tourism. The Knights Templar always protected, and in fact encouraged pilgrimages to sacred sites because such journeys to and from created commerce and allowed for the exchange of culture. Again, the aim of commerce was not simply business for business' sake. The main responsibility of the Knights Templar was to stimulate the exchange of energy, goods and services and to connect people so that they could appreciate and enjoy the beauty and the wonder of each other.

> **[Sidebar]** Tourism and travel are fantastic tools of commerce that help connect people around the world, creating revenue streams and spreading the wealth. Perhaps the Merchant Priests encouraged and fed people's fascination with the Grail by moving the rumors about its location around Europe intentionally, much as the Olympic Committee moves the flaming torch around the world today. Witness the great celebration in a city when it is awarded the Winter Olympics, for example. Not only is it a great honor to host top athletes from around the world, the flood of tourists and money that follow the Olympic Games is a great boon to the local economy. Meanwhile, the whole world party-cipates, gathering by the millions in front of their television sets.

Merlin's vision of the Holy Grail seeded society with a mythology that still vibrates in our hearts today. *The DaVinci Code* phenomenon was fueled by the burning desire to finally capture and claim the secret of the Grail. After all these years and all this searching and still the relic has eluded our efforts to acquire it at last and hold it up for all of humanity to see. Dan

Brown owes much of the success of his book to this odd conundrum, and even more to Merlin, one of history's most influential Merchant Priests. No doubt we will see ever more stories and spins on the theme of the Holy Grail. Humans have an insatiable appetite for truth, and the Grail is one of our strongest images for that which rests at our very core: the Immaculate Heart of Love.

Merlin knew that Great Britain, being an island, had unique potential to develop a culture that could emerge on the world stage as the bastion of the Merchant Priest's ideology. This is why so much energy was given to the myth as a spiritual current and a tool to advance chivalry in the community during the middle ages. The power of myth to shape the hearts and minds of men was well understood by the Merchant Priests. The tales of King Arthur are a pure example of how myth is employed to infuse culture with stories and legends that fire the collective imagination and encourage people to ponder higher values and, in the process, raise humanity to new heights.

The Prophet Mohammad's Part

Mohammad was a warrior who brought peace and prosperity to his people. By all accounts he was a humble and generous man who lived a short life filled with glory and tragedy. The founder of the Islamic tradition met his adored wife Khadijah while taking a trading caravan across the desert. This once orphaned boy was only 24 at the time and had already displayed characteristics that would mark him out in history. His strong sense of social justice was made apparent in his dealings as a Merchant. This was coupled with an interest in diverse intellecttual/emotional and spiritual matters and an innate ability to bring about reconciliation in the most difficult situations. Khadijah was a number of years his senior and a successful merchant in her own right. She proposed marriage and he accepted, thereby entering into the most important relationship of his life. She was his wife and mentor, schooling him in the ways of the Merchant Priesthood.

When asked by his companions the question of whom he loved most in the whole world, Mohammad always answered "Âishah" (his second wife, who he took after his first wife Khadijah died). For them it was deeply surprising to hear him announce love for a woman. This was a new concept for them, having always thought of love in terms of the manly camaraderie between warriors. So they asked him which man he loved most. He answered "Abû Bakr" (Âishah's father), a gentleman who was known for his sensitivity. These answers confounded his companions who until then had been brought up on patriarchal values. Mohammad was introducing reverence for the Feminine to them for the first time. His enemies taunted him about the fact that he had no sons, only daughters, while they had been given sons to perpetuate their patriarchal ways. Allah consoled the Prophet with a message: "We have given thee al-Kawthar." al-Kawthar (a sacred pool of life-giving water in Paradise—a profoundly feminine symbol) represented a heavenly exaltation of the Feminine over patriarchal society. Kawthar is derived from the same root as kathîr "abundance," a quality of the Divine Feminine.

A big part of Mohammad's teaching was about returning the sacred and the feminine to a culture where chauvinism and warrior mentality had overtaken society. After his own awakening Mohammad would go on to preach in the Holy Qur'an "None honors women except he who is honorable, and none despises them except he who is despicable" ... "The best of you is the one who is best toward women"... "Woman is the world's finest treasure."

> [Sidebar] Islam is often portrayed as a masculine patriarchal faith when actually the opposite is true if one researches the essence of the teachings. If you really look at Mohammad's teaching you will find the central importance of the feminine in the original teachings of Islam and will realize that it has been there from the beginning. Recently there has been a lot of controversy over how to re-shape Christianity to include the feminine on the divine level, but in Islam it has never been an issue since it was present from the beginning, especially in Sufism.

Mohammad settled in Mecca, a town made sacred by the Ka'bah. The Ka'bah—a black rock that was said to have fallen from the sky in the time of Abraham—was housed in a covered building. Along the building's side stood the many different deities of the warring tribes of Arabia. Because it was the major center of trade and communication for Arabia, Mecca was one of the few places where a longstanding truce had been enacted.

Tribes could worship their individual totems and observe their rites and rituals within the city in peace.

Mohammad enjoyed the varied pilgrims and merchants for whom the Ka'bah was a destination, and his reputation as an arbitrator of disputes grew. He also enjoyed an on-going dialogue between the many Christian and Jewish scholars and mystics whom he befriended.

Mohammad also spent much time alone wondering the hills above the bustling town and meditating in the Cave of Hira. It was here that Mohammad experienced Allah/God and the teachings and beauty that became the Holy Qur'an. In Arabic Allah has no form and is neither masculine nor feminine. Rather it is conceived as the perfect, omnipotent, omniscient, originating, and underlying force of the universe. It was Mohammad's experience of this that would start a revolution of tolerance, unity, forgiveness, trust, and beauty that would spread through faith and commerce to three continents and eventually the world.

Mohammad, a man of his time, was awake and aware of the needs and feelings of the people and the religious currents of his era. Divisions were deep and damaging in the tribal culture of Arabia and Mohammad's experience of the oneness of all beings enabled a new way of thinking and responding to life's challenges. His emphasis lay always in the unity of all, thereby creating acceptance, trust, connectedness, and beauty as a basis of existence. A merchant's life and livelihood was dramatically improved by the embodiment of these qualities, which when coupled with commerce spawned the vibrant, diverse, and ground-breaking Islamic culture. Mohammad held a dream similar to Akhenaten's, the dream of a spiritual society connected through commerce and united by one God.

For the most part the spread of Islam was welcomed by the people as a liberation from oppressive rulers and an overblown priesthood. Muslims were careful not to break down local cultures or lore, practicing only tolerance. But Islam allowed a direct connection to divinity, sparing the people's precious resources from a gorged and greedy clergy. Where ever they went they maintained, improved or established infrastructure. They built mosques, schools, and hospitals and created great beauty. *"Above all things Allah is beauty and thus beauty is transcendent."*

On his deathbed, Mohammad recommended to his followers to choose the best amongst them to lead after him. He made it clear that it was merit rather than bloodline that was the key to leadership. What he was advocating was the concept of "meritocracy" vs. full democracy, knowing that fully developed democracy could not be achieved before certain levels of prosperity, education, and emotional maturity have been achieved.

The Purpose of the Islamic State suggested by Mohammad clearly states that the aim is the establishment, maintenance and development of those virtues which the Creator of the universe wishes human life to be enriched by. The state in Islam is not intended for political administration, nor for the fulfillment of the collective will of any particular set of people. The aim is to encourage the qualities of purity, beauty, goodness, virtue, success and prosperity, which Allah wants to flourish in the life of the people while avoiding exploitation and injustice. To achieve this, the state must use all means at its disposal. In addition to placing before us this high ideal, Islam clearly states the desired virtues and the undesirable evils.

The Knights Templar

One of the most significant historical bridges the Merchant Priests used to pass the baton through the ages from Egypt to now is the Knights Templar. With the decline of Egypt, the mantel was handed to the Hebrews and the energy current carried by the Priesthood was transferred to a special order of knights. Born in the Middle Ages, this sect is perhaps the best example of a holy order of monastic warriors whose discipline was the unification of sacred and secular activities within the context of banking and trading. Again, as with the Egyptians, these men knew that commerce was a path to the sacred heart when practiced in a sacred context.

The Knights Templar did more than we, or they, will ever know to usher us into the world we know today. They were the real life counterparts to King Arthur's knights. As peace-brokers for kings and popes alike, they were the embodiments of the Holy Grail. Among their ranks noble blood always gave deference to merit, thus usurping the old paradigm wherein power was passed down from above. In the spiritual (versus religious) paradigm, the only hierarchy that exists is the hierarchy of love and support. Bloodlines and "the divine right of kings" no longer reigns supreme. Mutual consideration and courtesy are high values to the emergent class of men who, in turn, become concerned with being "gentle-men" and protecting the people. Having assumed the mission of protecting the pilgrim routes to Jerusalem, their reputation was and is unique in the annals of history. The Knights Templar exemplified balance of character in one man where the perfect harmony suggested by the yin-yang symbol is given expression in the gentleness of a lamb and the ferocity of a lion.

The Templars' origins can be traced to Hugues de Payens who traveled east to the Holy Land during the Christian crusades in the early part of the 12th century. Originally a vassal to Count Hugh of Champagne, de Payens stayed in Jerusalem when Count Hugh returned to France. The richest of the feudal lords at that time, Count Hugh was reportedly four to five times wealthier than the king of France. He was strongly influenced by a religious form of mysticism and reformist Benedictine thought. On their pilgrimage to Jerusalem, Count Hugh and de Paynes encountered the Muslim concept of chivalry—the Bedouin principles of al-furusiyyah (horsemanship) and muru'ah (manliness and honor), which emphasize brotherhood, courage, generosity, and loyalty.

In the deserts of Arabia, a man in Arab dress—sword in scabbard and spear in hand, riding his pure Arabian across the sands—has long since been a symbol of justice and protection. Since time immemorial, the chivalrous Arabian knight protected his womenfolk; he was the prototype for the medieval western knight in shining armor. From long before the birth of Christ prior to the advent of Islam, chivalry was a recognized social institution on the Arabian Peninsula. The Arabs are said to have been among the first to practice a chivalrous code of honor as a way of life.

Unlike the Greeks, Romans and Persians, Arab wars were fought fairly and, for the most part, without treachery. Champions fought before both armies, and battles often took place by appointment. Arabian chivalry was a code of ethics, life and social structure that grew until it became synonymous with the quest for freedom and justice as well as a man fighting to the death to protect the women and children. Protecting the good repute and honor of women, family and tribe was a basic requirement for an Arabian knight. In pre- and early Islam, women were very important in society. They inspired the poet to sing and the warrior to fight. Knights were not formally knighted as later was the custom in Europe; they became knights by reputation. Their courage, dignity and noble deeds made them treasures to their people. Their adventures and feats were the subject of many tales and legends.

Count Hugh returned to France and sent nine of his vassals back to the Temple Mount in Jerusalem. Convinced that he himself carried the bloodline of Jesus, the Count charged his vassals with the task of unearthing the secrets inside the Ark of the Covenant. Ever a subject of intrigue and mystery, the Ark had been carried out of Egypt by Moses, eventually made its way to Jerusalem, and was buried or lost when the Temple of Solomon fell in 586 BC.

The Temple Mount in Jerusalem was the spiritual center of the Middle East. The Wailing Wall finds the Hebrew people worshipping on one side, and the Muslims streaming into the Mosque on the other. Count Hugh's vassals, who became the Knights Templar, spent ten years fulfilling their assignment to dig beneath the Temple Mount in search of the Ark and its secrets. Eventually, Hugh gave up his title and his wife and went to Jerusalem to join the search and what became the Templar Order. Templar records always speak of hidden treasure, not the jewels and gold coins variety, but treasure in the form of secret knowledge. It is believed that the treasured Ark was safely spirited away when Jerusalem fell in 1291. The earliest written copies of Masonic ritual claim that the Ark was found in a cave on the Temple Mount.

Over the next two hundred years, the Order of the Poor Knights of Christ and the Temple of Solomon—the "Knights Templar," for short—became the most powerful and secretive organization in history. They amassed great wealth and owed allegiance to none but the Pope. Many features of the international money exchange system originated with the Templars;

kings of Europe were indebted to the Order. Chapters functioned as schools of diplomacy, with advanced degrees in commerce and finance. The vast estates owned by the Order were sanctuaries for all who needed protection. Individual knights took vows of poverty and did not accumulate personal wealth. Instead, they used their wealth to leverage land deals and make advances in agriculture. They supported new construction, building expansion and the modest beginnings of industry. Charged with ensuring safe passage to those making a pilgrimage to the Holy Land from Europe, they devised a system utilizing a coded chit that is a clear precursor to the modern day credit card. In short, they put their wealth to work in service of the whole.

Exempt from excommunication and all papal decrees not specifically addressed to them, the Templars also managed to free themselves from any tax liability. As "defenders of church and cross" they became a separate social, political, and religious order that transcended all legal and economic lines. Although their military presence in the east diminished once the Muslims reclaimed Jerusalem, the Templars' influence at the local level was strong. The Order had thousands of houses around Europe. They were business managers, farm and vineyard owners, and held safe deposit boxes where people stored their valuables and wealth. Their unique status as a sovereign state with a standing army that knew no borders was a source of great tension, especially with the king of France who had amassed a sizeable debt to the Order while warring with England.

In an attempt to resolve this tension and erase his debt, King Phillip the Fair of France devised a plan to merge all the religious orders—including the Templars—and form the Knights of Jerusalem with a French prince at the helm. When his "merger and acquisitions" plan failed, King Phillip launched a massive campaign against the Templars, accusing them of magic and heresy. On October 13, 1307 Phillip the Fair had every Templar in France arrested; some stories say the arrests occurred at a grand party hosted by the king. The sudden demise of the Templars, whose goodwill and protection the common people had come to depend on, sent a ripple effect across Europe that fed and accelerated the eventual collapse of the monarchy. Over the course of the next five years, hundreds of Knights were tortured and put to death, executed by fire or imprisoned. The last Grand Master, Jacques de Molay, was burnt at the stake in 1314.

To escape persecution by King Philip of France, the Templars' treasure and their enormous fleet of ships disappeared. History books describe how the Templars were in possession of a mysterious "great secret." Historical data about the Ark of the Covenant is difficult to come by and theories about its disappearance and whereabouts abound.

What we find most fascinating is that the men who went in search of it founded an order that rose to great power and prominence in the years that followed. They abandoned their search for the bloodline of Christ, created a chivalrous order of knights inspired by their experience of chivalry amongst the Arabian knights, and instead went about doing good works that brought greater prosperity to much of Europe.

Could it be that they actually found the secrets of the Merchant Priesthood, some special knowledge that made it out of Egypt and can be traced as the spiritual current we are calling Sacred Commerce? Perhaps what they discovered was not a bloodline, but instructions on how to align their activities with the implicit divine order. Would that not explain how they amassed such great wealth and power in the years that followed? And what if their activities even then favored freeing the masses from the oppression of poverty and war rather than supporting the sole authority of church or crown? Might this explain why they were such a clear threat to the existing power structure that both the French crown and the Pope rallied to strip them of the power passed down to them through Moses from Akhenaten?

Many claim that this "great secret" if revealed may undermine our fundamental view of Christianity. Although some see this to mean the real story of the bloodline of Jesus and the mysteries of Mary Magdalene and the sacred feminine in Christianity, my belief is that they discovered the secret of Emotional Alchemy for personal transformation and transcendence, the secrets and highest truth of spirituality—that we create our own reality rather a preordained destiny and that one can have a direct and unique relationship and partnership with the divine rather than just through organized religion.

It is generally assumed that the Order ended with Grand Master Jacques de Molay's death. However, some of the Knights Templar managed to escape the purges in France. A fleet of some twenty ships sailed off to Scotland and there found safe harbor. Robert the Bruce, then King of Scotland, had been excommunicated by Rome and did not answer to the Pope or fall under his jurisdiction. Soon after the Templars' arrival, Masonic guilds began appearing all over Scotland.

[Sidebar] We'd like to dispel some of the suspicion around the Masons and other so-called secret societies. Although there were power-hungry secret societies, this does not mean they all were. Many were uniquely benevolent. Seen through the lens of evolution, certain individuals were involved in a specialized training that made them more adept at carrying the torch of awareness forward. Those with special training and knowledge went "underground" (or "below the radar," in modern terms), concealing what they knew or working behind the scenes during "dark" times when prevailing beliefs as promoted by the ruling class or the church sought to extinguish the light of awareness—be that basic literacy, the tools of commerce, or a democratic mind-set.

Another group of Knights managed to escape and travel east to Switzerland, taking their knowledge and treasure with them. As luck or the Divine Plan would have it, their escape coincided with Switzerland's formation as a conglomeration of provinces. The early Swiss records speak of the mysterious appearance of white knights that helped the local population gain their independence from foreign domination. The Templar cross is incorporated still today in many of the flags of the Swiss cantons, as are two other prominent Templar symbols: keys and the lamb. In settling in Switzerland the Templars had a significant impact on it becoming the banking and global finance center that it continues to be even today.

The Knights Templar inherited an unbroken line of technical knowledge. Indeed, the Merchant Priesthood—here manifest as an order of Knights—always carried the keys in the form of the latest technological know-how. In early times, as now on the Internet, navigation was crucial (see Google sidebar below). While we swap domains and servers and Internet access points, they owned large fleets and elaborate maps. Long before the development of the chronometer, they were able to circumnavigate the world due to their ability to fix longitudinal positions. Some of their ships—along with their knowledge and principles—reached Nova Scotia years before Columbus reached the Americas. Some historians believe that Isaac Newton, Vasco De Gama and Columbus himself had connections to the Order. Some evidence even suggests that the Templars discovered America some 80 years before Columbus.

[Sidebar] Consider the remarkable success of Google; this visionary company is clearly aligned with the aims of the Merchant Priesthood. More than any single search engine on the Internet, Google has leveled the playing field by giving everyone the ability to navigate the world wide web and access more information than ever before in history. At the same time it has allowed people to monetize their information, experience and creations, providing a new avenue for abundance to flow. Consider innovations like eBay and online shopping carts that afford everyone the ability to become an international merchant. As we work toward completion of this manuscript, Google is in the process of scanning every page of every book in every library, thus making the knowledge in those libraries accessible to the furthest corners of the world at the touch of a button.

It seems highly likely that the Templars had early contact with the Native American Iroquois nation in Canada. Legend tells of them contributing to the Iroquois "Great Law of Peace"—a democratic system of checks and balances between the tribes that helped to maintain general peace. Benjamin Franklin learned of this indigenous constitution and allowed it to influence his thinking in the writing of the American Constitution. So, the Templars influenced the Iroquois, who in turn carried the seed, added their wisdom and experience, and handed it on to the next great experiment in democracy, the United States of America.

[Sidebar] The "Great Law of Peace" Confederacy arose centuries ago among separate, warring communities as a way to create harmony, unity, and respect among human beings. Implicit in Iroquois political philosophy is commitment to the highest principles of human liberty. The Iroquois Law's recognition of individual liberty and justice surpasses any European parallel. Faithkeeper Oren Lyons, in Onondaga, states The Great Law of Peace includes "freedom of speech, freedom of religion, [and] the right of women to participate in government. Separation of power in government and checks and balances within government are traceable to our Iroquois constitution—ideas learned by colonists."

The central idea underlying Iroquois political philosophy is that peace is the will of the Creator and the ultimate spiritual goal and natural order among humans. The principles of Iroquois government embodied in The Great Law of Peace were transmitted by a historical figure called the Peacemaker. His teachings emphasize the power of Reason to assure Righteousness, Justice and Health among humans. Peace came to the Iroquois, not through war and conquest, but through the exercise of Reason guided by the spiritual mind. The Iroquois League is based not on force of arms or rule of law, but spiritual concepts of natural law applied to human society.

The Iroquois were not the only indigenous Americans to play a part in world affairs. The Incas also played a key role in the establishment of capitalism when they flooded Spain and the rest of Europe with silver. When Spanish conquistadors went to Peru in search of gold, the Merchant Priests of the Inca's conspired to open them to the Silver Mountain. For centuries, legend told of the Peruvian shamans telling their people to leave the vast stores of this rare mineral they had found in the earth untouched; they foresaw a time when the silver would be needed for a higher purpose. That time came.

The Incan shamans led the Spanish to a virtual mountain of silver and shortly thereafter the mineral began pouring into Europe. Gold was the main currency up until that time and was nearly exclusively in the hands of royalty and the church; everybody else bartered with sheep, crops, crafts, services, or whatever they had. By introducing silver in industrial quantities—a feminine, cooling energy—the Merchant Priests sought to balance the overheated gold-standard economy. In time silver became a cheap form of universal currency for the emerging bourgeois classes. This development was absolutely necessary for capitalizing new ideas and developing new products, giving birth to the middle class that later bankrolled democracy in France and parts of Europe. The Merchant Priesthood could thus pass the baton—with a middle class in place the people began to champion and protect their democracy. This duplicated the earlier passing on of responsibility that occurred when the Merchant Priesthood introduced another cultural innovation—agriculture—and gave that practice to the people as a tool to meet their basic survival needs. Coins and currency are of little interest when having enough food is the primary issue as it was in earlier times.

These two examples—agriculture and currency—demonstrate the role played by the Merchant Priesthood in sculpting a balanced society. Although their presence among the Incas cannot be tracked historically, this move by men of their priestly class certainly evidences a rarified sensibility and understanding of collective human behavior and economics. The introduction of silver as a fully integrated currency mitigated the appetite for gold in Europe at a time when gold fever was heating up the economy. A beautiful illustration of our interdependence with the mineral kingdoms, silver in effect cooled down the collective psychic state of Europeans. This effectively shifted the economic base to the people; no longer was the aristocracy the exclusive holders of the purse strings. As we have seen, any time we effectively "level the playing field" in this manner, we pave the way for increasingly greater democracy. Important to note in this context that the introduction of silver eventually supported the creation of capitalism—the invention that eventually bankrolled democracy.

Tulip Mania:
The First Great Market Bubble

One of the great stories in the history of commerce is the tulip mania that seized the Netherlands circa 1630. What few understand is that the Merchant Priesthood was behind the scene. This time they worked with the plant kingdom; among their allies were potatoes and tulips.

The water mains in Northern Europe were liberated when farmers began to plant potatoes instead of wheat (a water intensive crop). The water that had previously been monopolized by agriculture became available for an entirely new phenomenon: generating electricity. As the Industrial Revolution began its gestation period, France, Holland and Germany, each in their own way, started sending out ships to colonize what they considered "the territories."

Fighting between France and England started to block—and in some cases, even destroy—the trade routes. Previously, trade had flowed freely, but with imperialism on the rise and European powers intent on monopolizing the world, trade routes were cut and shortened, inhibiting commerce. Excessive demand in Europe made supplies elsewhere scarce.

The Merchant Priesthood in the Ottoman Empire responded to a request from their South African brothers who were suffering at the hands of the Dutch. Together, they devised an unusually clever intervention—a plan that would nudge down Holland's GNP (Gross National Product, a measure of the wealth of a nation). Their aim was to reduce the available capital the Dutch had to finance their imperialistic ambitions. They decided to introduce something entirely new in the European economy. This move was not so much an economic ploy to hijack their excess wealth as it was a means to re-distribute it.

The Merchant Priests also sought to tame and balance the self-importance of the European powers as their emotional inflation was threatening to monopolize global trade.

When a leading botanist from Leiden went on a trade visit to Constantinople, he had no idea of the mellifluous adventure on which he was about to embark. The tulip mania he was about to trigger is often cited in histories of collective mania and obsession. The effects of the tulip flower were actually well-known in ancient Greece where they were used in the Elysian Mysteries to bring on temporary amnesia.

The Merchant Priesthood knew that if the tulip flower made its way to Europe, one of two things would happen. Either the delicate perfume of the flower would serve to calm the collective economic and emotional frenzy of the times, or the population would become obsessed with the flower. In the case of the later, they foresaw people becoming so obsessed with acquisition of the tulip flower that this would cause a speculative bubble that would eventually crash. Either way, they knew that a certain amount of financial heat would be taken out of the system.

The notion of a flower scent being so powerful as to affect an entire culture might seem rather far-fetched. Certainly, a huge quantity of the blooming anomaly would be required to have an effect. But consider the current fascination with flower essences, essential oils, and aromatherapy, or even the vast marketing budgets the cosmetic industry puts behind their newest *Passion* or *Taboo*. In this light, the thought of a flower having hypnotic olfactory power over people becomes less absurd.

The tulip bulb was brought north to Europe just after the turn of the 16th century. Within a few short decades the flower was in high demand all across the continent. By the 1630s the demand had reached a fever pitch. In the Netherlands people were selling everything they had to purchase a few bulbs. At the peak of the bubble one humble tulip bulb was selling for the equivalent of 20 tons of cheese! A 17th century father might have trouble finding a suitor for his daughter if the tulip was not prominent in her dowry. For a few years the bulbs themselves became an alternative form of currency, often traded like stocks at the mansion of an aristocrat in Amsterdam whose name was La Bourse. To this day the Paris Stock Exchange bears his name.

> **[Sidebar]** In one of the most popular novels of the 1800s Alexander Dumas tells the tale of The Black Tulip. Set in the Netherlands city of Haarlem, the novel tells of fierce competition between the country's best gardeners for a prize of 100,000 florins (600k shillings) promised to the person who could grow a black tulip. Truly black flowers are unknown in nature, and yet, twentieth century black tulips—the African Queen, Black Diamond, Black Hero, and Arabian Mystery, which are actually deep shades of ruby-red, mahogany, burgundy wine, and violet purple—evoke a sense of lusty drama to this very day.

This flurry of economic activity had a number of downstream effects that demonstrate the unusual role of the Merchant Priesthood in cultural evolution. As we have said before, this unique ministry had its sights less on "saving souls" and more on providing tools for commerce that allow the poorer segments of society to rise above poverty and enjoy abundance and prosperity. How did tulip mania serve these ends? In effect, it led to the first futures market, which eventually gave birth to the stock market.

The stock market allows people with small amounts of capital to invest and get onto a larger playing field, a privilege formerly reserved for big capital. This innovation allows the individual to gain from the success of large companies creating a participatory economy that lets many levels of society prosper. As an example let's look at what happens when a large company sells shares or stock. They raise money by selling to millions of small shareholders, which allows the workingman to participate in the success and abundance generated by big capital. The small investor is the progeny of the stock market. One share gives him a voice; he can now participate in a larger commercial activity than were he to work solely on his own. The stock market is also a tool that allows entrepreneurs with new ideas and innovations to raise needed capital. This in turn also redistributes wealth because the rich are not the only ones who can get richer; the middle class can grow their bank accounts, portfolios and assets as well.

Just how did the lovely tulip flower set off this domino effect? Because the flowers were imported from Crete it took quite a long time for them to get to Northern Europe. Shipments were purchased in advance, creating the first "futures market." It was not at all uncommon for 60-90% of the tulips to die in transit, which meant the price could go up or down by as much as ten times. In effect, the futures market has always been an economic betting game, or in this case tulip roulette. Among both the aristocracy and the emerging middle class, people were so hot to obtain the coveted flower that many sold off their assets at below market price in order to speculate on the tulip market. The poorer sections of society benefited from this dumping of assets.

In 1637 the tulip speculation bubble burst. The heat of the European economy began to cool—all because of the ingenuity and the enchantment wafting up from a brightly colored bloom.

Did the Merchant Priesthood really think all this out and strategically plan such interventions? Was the process that conscious, or more of an unconscious movement toward an idea that held some vague promise of merit? Perhaps we will never know if silver currency and tulip mania were pre-conceived as a "big plan" or if they just acted on what they knew and felt to do in the moment. What we mean to highlight is simple: the spiritual current toward higher forms of both individual and collective expression has moved humanity throughout time. We affectionately call this current "the Pulse," and experience its flow and elegant movement in a personal way that might be called "destiny."

The Founding of America

The principles of the Merchant Priesthood also played a pivotal role in the founding of America; it was to be their greatest experiment and achievement. With the birth of the United States the new form of governance known as democracy gained considerable velocity. Thirteen of the 39 signatories of the Constitution were Freemasons; nine Masons were among the group who drew up the Declaration of Independence.

This document carries a message much like that of the French Revolution with its slogan of Liberty, Fraternity and Equality. American revolutionaries added the spiritual dimension to their dream by including "the pursuit of happiness." As Maslow points out with the Hierarchy of Needs pyramid, each time you satisfy a need you become happier. Happiness arises with the fulfillment of our needs from survival to beauty and is the essence of enlightenment, or *the realized self* in Maslow's terms.

Common to both the French and the American revolutions was the goal of establishing a republican form of governance that would feature a congress and president elected by the people. These ideals bear witness to the influence of the Freemasons who saw themselves as architects of a new Temple of Solomon, which was destroyed in AD 70 by the Roman Emperor Titus. Among the Freemasons the Temple symbolized the "New Jerusalem"—the finest and most rarified expression of human nature possible. With the opening of America, the Freemasons resurfaced. It is no coincidence that Washington D.C. has always been known as the shining city on the hill!

Neither is it a coincidence that the dollar bill shows a truncated pyramid with the cap not yet quite in place. The All Seeing Eye of Wisdom that beams out from the cap will finally be in place when the United States of America is governed and led by the spiritual ideals that were encoded into its founding documents.

Much of this symbolic communication was the work of the Freemasons. They had great hopes for the United States. Considering their history and the persecution of the Knights Templar by King Philip of France, it is easy to understand their allegiance to a republican form of government that adheres to the principles of democracy. Those who crafted the documents that formed this nation truly believed that America had the potential to become the country where secular and sacred power could finally be clearly separated, thus their strong support of the First Amendment and religious tolerance.

Given the deeply spiritual intent of the Founding Fathers, the notion of separating church and state always struck me as something of an oxymoron. What I now realize is that their focus was on "church and state," NOT "spirituality and state." How can governance unfold benevolently without divine guidance and influence? What seems true is that the aim was not so much to separate the secular and the sacred as it was to create a roadblock for the government from exercising control over people's spirituality. The treachery we saw in France and other parts of Europe when Royalty was in cahoots with the Church highlighted the folly of mixing these two bedfellows. We still see examples of this around the world. If spiritual development is the main goal in a person's life they naturally want to make that dimension of existence available to others. The Founding Fathers aimed at keeping the sphere of spirituality unencumbered. They had a deep sense of spirituality and believed strongly that each individual should have the right to their own unique relationship with God, not controlled by the State or the Church. The Founding Fathers championed spiritual sovereignty by declaring freedom of choice with respect to whatever godhead one might conceive or implore. In business dealings there is no need for separation between spiritual and secular. In fact, business can be an accelerated spiritual path. As a feedback mechanism that reveals our thoughts and feelings, beliefs and attitudes, and choices and decisions, the business world is second to none. In failure and success our business activities not only speed up the flow of information, they diversify the information that comes back to us. The multiplicity of relationships that Sacred Commerce brings into our lives compels us to work more consciously to stay in balance and grow.

Benjamin Franklin was a celebrated member of the Freemasons and a Grand Master at the age of 28. One of the best known Founding Fathers of America, he was also an inventor, diplomat, civic activist, and political and social engineer. In 1727 at the age of 21 he founded the first volunteer association in America, the *Junto*. This lively discussion group was convened to bring together aspiring artisans and tradesmen who shared a commitment to improving themselves while they improved their community. As the first "convention" of this kind, the Junto can be seen as the precursor to the entire self-help and personal growth movement. Their focus on what we would call "inner and outer ecology" in today's world is what made the Junto both unique and effective. Philadelphia's volunteer fire department and many other civic-minded service organizations grew out of this group. Franklin also founded the first public library in America, a vision that spread across the land resulting in thousands of libraries gracing even the smallest community. Again, we see the expression of the Merchant Priesthood's mission to level the playing field and bring resources—in this case knowledge and literacy—to the people.

From his late twenties and throughout his thirties (the "midlife" years by 18th century standards) Franklin's trade was that of a printer. In effect, he was an author and publisher—best known for the famous *Poor Richard's Almanac* (still in print over two centuries later) and *The Pennsylvania Gazette*. His eloquent writings significantly contributed to the ideals of democracy and are among the most important works of political theory and philosophy we have.

Franklin was born into a world where suspicion, witch-hunts, and slavery dominated human thought—a world where a lightning strike was seen as punishment from the hand of God and where a man was expected to simply accept his station in life. In Franklin's case, that meant a life of poverty as a member of the working class. But Franklin's soul force and unique genius propelled him far beyond the limitations of his birth and the dominant view of reality at the time. A wealthy man by the age of 30, Franklin made innumerable contributions to 18th century society, not the least of which was protection from the hand of God when it came down from the sky with supreme vengeance.

> **[Sidebar]** In those days if a lightning bolt struck a house or farm, it was seen as punishment due—a clear indication that the owner had committed some sin. The community would protect the neighboring homes from fire and simply let the house struck by lightning burn to the ground. When he invented the lightning rod, Franklin not only provided protection, he shook the very foundation of the prevailing chauvinistic worldview that presupposes an absolute and punishing authority lording over us from on high. If freewill allows us to protect ourselves from the hand of God, what else might we do with this marvelous capacity? How else can we work in partnership with the powers that be?

What is important to note about Franklin's life in the context of Sacred Commerce is his generosity and "gift-economy" attitude. Although he was a copious inventor, Franklin never patented so much as one of his inventions—not out of martyrdom or lack of interest in his own financial well-being, but out of his zeal to speed the evolution of his countrymen and his desire to have impact. He was a special breed of entrepreneur as can be seen in the following statement from his autobiography: "[A]s we enjoy great advantages from the invention of others, we should be glad of an opportunity to serve others by any invention of ours; and this we should do freely and generously."

By creating a bastion for democracy on the continent of North America, the Freemasons took a stand for freedom—economic freedom, intellectual freedom, and spiritual freedom—the dream of the Merchant Priesthood.

Today's Knights of Commerce
The Rise of the Global Citizen

"The ones who are crazy enough to think that they can change the world, are the ones who do."
--Steve Jobs

Today's Merchant Priests may not know themselves by that name or as the "Knights of Commerce," but they are men and women changing the face of society and humanity by leveling the playing field in new and innovative ways. We will look at just a couple of them as examples. We know there are many more; maybe you are one of them!

Dr. Mohammad Yunus is one of the first economists and bankers to sit in the company of Nelson Mandela, the Dalai Lama, Desmond Tutu, Mother Teresa and others whose work has advanced the cause of peace.

As a university professor, Dr. Yunus wondered why economic theory had so little to do with the reality of slow economic growth in poor nations like his own—Bangladesh. In 1974 he met a young craftswoman who made lovely bamboo stools. Due to the fact that she was not an "independent contractor" (to use our terms) but instead had to rely on someone else to provision her with bamboo, the woman could only earn two cents per day. With a simple $6 loan, Dr. Yunus helped her to rise up to middle class by increasing her daily income to $1.25. That six dollars, in effect, allowed her to go into business for herself.

In 1979 he founded the first micro lending bank—a bank whose focus was loaning small amounts of money to people in the poor rural areas, primarily women. The Grameen Bank not only lends money to the poor, it is also majority-owned by the borrowers themselves. Their success has been phenomenal. By 1996 they had loaned more in rural areas than all the other banks combined.

As of 2007, the Grameen Bank has 2,452 branches with 23,667 staff serving 7.24 million borrowers. Grameen collects an average of $1.5 million in weekly installments. Of the borrowers, 95% are women and over 98% of the loans are re-paid, a recovery rate higher than any other banking system. It currently lends close to half a billion dollars a year, and has loaned $6.38 billion to date. It is financially self-reliant, it does not take any loan or grant from any source. All its funds come from the deposits it collects from the borrowers and non-borrowers, and it routinely makes a profit.

This year, to explode the myth that microcredit does not work for the "bottom" poor, Grameen Bank launched a program to give loans exclusively to beggars, particularly generational beggars. The bank invites them to carry a collection of popular consumer items (financed by Grameen Bank) when they go out to beg. They can both beg and sell, their choice. Nearly 10,000 beggars have already joined the program. A typical loan to a beggar amounts to $10 US.

Dr. Yunus believes that we can create a poverty-free world, that the basic ingredient to overcome poverty is packed inside each poor person, and that all we need to do is to help the person to unleash their energy and creativity.

Credit is the last hope left to those faced with absolute poverty. That is why Muhammad Yunus believes that the right to credit should be recognized as a fundamental human right. His work goes far deeper than financial health. He is deeply involved in restoring the dignity, hope, and personal worth to people generally forgotten by society. His belief in them has inspired many others to believe in them as well, but most importantly it has inspired them to believe in themselves, a priceless gift.

The micro lending movement has spread from Bangladesh across the globe. After visiting some of the villages Paul Wolfowitz of the World Bank spoke out on the transformative potential of microfinance : "I thought maybe this was just one successful project in one village, but then I went to the next village and it was the same story. That evening I met with more than a hundred women leaders from self-help groups, and I realized this program was opening opportunities for poor women and their families in an entire state of 75 million people."

Dr. Yunus's personal dream is to see poverty and homelessness banished to legend, to be learned about only in museums and libraries.

One of the most successful business ventures on Earth began when a lone bank manager asked some tough questions that sparked a massive mutation in the practice of free enterprise. Every time you pull out your Visa card you participate in a quiet revolution that began in 1968 when one man led a historical move to level the playing field for merchants across the globe. When Dee Hock convinced Bank of America to relinquish ownership and control of their credit card program in favor of a non-stock membership company equally owned by its member banks, a new species of corporation began to evolve. Inducted into the both the Business Hall of Fame and *Money Magazine's* Hall of Fame, Dee Hock busted chauvinism's individualistic paradigm at the corporate level.

Decades before the birth of the Internet, he was one of the first Knights of E-Commerce. Like the Merchant Priest of old, Dee Hock did humanity a great service by paving the way for more equality in the marketplace. He developed the concept of a global system for the electronic exchange of value and a unique new form of organization for that purpose: a decentralized, non-stock, for-profit membership institution to be owned by financial institutions throughout the world.

Prior to the Bank Americard—predecessor to today's ticket-to-ride on the rails of commerce everywhere, your Visa card—only big vendors could do business in the credit card game. The local coffee shop or pottery store could only complete a transaction in cash or by accepting the ever-dubious personal check. A small machine that instantly approved and completed a financial transaction did not exist when the flower children of the 60s came of age. Hock's curiosity and courage changed all that. Today, a single mother who makes quilts and kids pajamas in her spare time can readily set up a vendor booth at a music festival and sell her wares to anyone who holds a Visa card.

The world wide success of Visa International, Dee Hock asserts, is due to its chaotic structure. At the time of publishing his book, "The Birth of the Chaordic Age" (1999), Visa was owned by 22,000 member banks, which both compete with each other for 750 million customers and must cooperate by honoring one another's $1.25 trillion transactions annually across borders and currencies. Today the Visa organization that Hock founded is not only performing brilliantly, it is also almost mythic, one of only two examples that experts regularly cite to illustrate how the dynamic principles of chaos theory can be applied to business.

This move was not unlike the creation of coin and currency that birthed the middle class and fostered a new wave of merchants that expanded the domain of mercantilism. We now see yet another wave of this type with the creation of eBay, PayPal, and shopping carts that make it easy to conduct commerce via the Internet.

The Internet offers the most challenging and exciting opportunity the human race has ever encountered; it is the means by which we may finally be able to bring harmony, spiritual balance, and abundance to bear for all. By its very nature the Web demands collaboration, invites participation, and encourages autonomy simultaneously, allowing individual differences to be highlighted and monetized. Party-cipation provides the lubricant for collaboration, encouraging partnerships that coalesce and then dissolve with each new project. The Web opens us to the inevitability of change. It also propels the spread and deepens the ideal of democracy; in short order we may see democratic systems all across the globe. Some countries have tried to restrict the Internet since its inception, but those attempts are failing. Governments are realizing they have to choose between becoming part of the global village and allow their people to become global citizens, or miss the boat of cultural evolution.

Perhaps the most important feature introduced into society by the Internet is the element of transparency. Few are the secrets that hide beyond the reach of Google and YouTube. Who would have imagined an information age wherein a weapon of mass de-construction would bear a name like Firefox. Or where watchdogs like smokinggun.com or snopes.com would keep us abreast of the latest hoax, smokescreen or scandal. No hope, no prayer, not even the most elaborate cloaking device can hide from the public what is really happening when even ten-year-olds carry cellular phones with builtin video cameras in their hip pocket. Far from a police state, what we are witnessing is the emergence of a transparent and intimate state. Open, undisguised, and increasingly *honest* government becomes inevitable and all but unavoidable. A truly global citizenry looms large on our horizon.

Even the world's foremost Web analysts cannot predict where the Internet will take us. The medium itself is a blank screen. Like any technology, it is neither good nor evil, but rather reflective of how it is used. More and more the Internet reveals itself as the screen onto which we project our character, motivations, and dreams. Ultimately, as is true with any human creation, we shall simply behold our own reflection on the Internet. This is why, for the Knights of E-Commerce of Silicon Valley, it becomes so urgent to use the Web in those ways that further all that is most ennobling and human in us—that which facilitates prosperity, peace, and conscious evolution.

The way the Web reaches into everything is another clue to its potential universal, even spiritual, character. It is like nature in the manner that all things are interconnected. In this way—by relating all parts to a larger whole—the Web has realized an innate inclination towards "systems" and "ecological" principles.

The Web can tell us about the origins of a particular product, the research that went into it, or even the degree to which its production and constituents may have harmed life.

With the power of the Web at our fingertips, we can choose to become more aware of the values we are buying into when we purchase a product or service. We have an influence on the life of a product, given that our vote to buy or not to buy directly impacts a product's existence. "Knowledge is Freedom," the saying goes. The Web gives us the freedom of informed choice, puts us in the larger picture, and makes that larger picture available to anyone who asks—or Googles—the right questions. For this reason, the Web is a call to responsibility and to responsible choices. Above all, because of its equally great potential to deluge us with too much information, the Web is a wakeup call to our powers of discernment.

Finally, the Web has also helped to spread the impact and manifestation of the dream of the Merchant Priesthood well beyond its initial participants—indeed, well beyond those that consciously aspire to be of service.

Throughout history the Merchant Priests, whether men and women grouped in religious orders, monastic warriors, secret societies or as individual renaissance dreamers, shared a similar vision. They imagined a global economy that empowers local economies around the world—from the largest to the smallest—to prosper and flourish with dignity and equality. A global marketplace where the spirit of partnership and responsibility transforms emotions of anger, fear and jealousy into passion, compassion and empathy. Where the natural flow of information, ideas and resources between different segments of society and across cultures transcends the unconscious exchange of baseless commodities—uniting and exalting, rather than dividing, people around the world.

They dreamt of the rise of the global citizens movement to move the world closer to their ultimate dream of a global conscious evolution. They dreamt of global citizens all over the world party-cipating through Sacred Commerce and Philanthropy, creating a new world rather than fixing or changing the old one.

This spiritual vision of the future confirms the qualitative and quantitative research work of Paul Ray and Sherry Anderson. They documented a new phenomena—the rise of the Cultural Creatives and the global citizens. This new group of people challenge the modernist interpretation of the world (nation-state-centric, technology and progress will solve the day, environment is important but security more so) and the traditional view of the world (strong patriarchy, strong religion, strong culture, agriculture-based and derived). Ray and Anderson go so far as to say that up to 25% of those in OECD (Organization for Economic Co-operation and Development) nations now subscribe to the spiritual/eco/gender partnership/global governance/alternative to capitalism position (www.culturalcreatives.org). However, they clearly state that Cultural Creatives or global citizens do not associate themselves with a political or social movement. Indeed, they represent a paradigm change, a change in values.

Oxfam defines Global Citizens as individuals who are aware of the wider world and have a sense of their own role as a world citizen. They respect and value diversity, have an understanding of how the world works economically, politically and socially, and are outraged by social injustice. They are willing to act to make the world a more sustainable and caring place and to take full responsibility for their actions. They recognize the interdependence of all people and, through cooperative effort, they make a difference in their community and their world.

In most discussions the global citizens movement is a sociopolitical process rather than a political organization or party structure. Sometimes the term is used synonymously with the anti-globalization movement. Not that the global citizens are against the ideal of globalization, but they know from their own experience of history that multinationals and government in general can misuse this ideal. They are against the creation of a world government, and the blending together of cultures creating a monoculture based mainly on western ideals and unsustainable consumerism. They have decided to take action and participate.

[Sidebar] Some of the earliest recorded material found on the concept of a global citizen first emerged among the Greek Cynics in the 4th Century BC, who coined the term "cosmopolitan" – meaning citizen of the world. The Roman Stoics later elaborated on the concept. The contemporary concept of cosmopolitanism, which proposes that all individuals belong to a single moral community, has gained a new salience as scholars examine the ethical requirements of the planetary phase of civilization.

Millions of humans across every important sector of business today are working for a more abundant, conscious world. They may not be consciously aware that they are indeed manifesting the values of the spiritual current of the Merchant Priesthood in their practice of Conscious Living, Right Livelihood, Emotional Intelligence, and party-cipatory philanthropy

Party-cipatory philanthropy is a philanthropy that is sourced in empathy, rather than sympathy, and in joy rather than guilt .It is about people coming together to create change, actively participating in projects and watching them grow. Party-cipatory philanthropy requires the individual to take full responsibility for the direction and impact of the service/contribution provided

Global Citizens like Lynn Twist, author of *The Soul of Money*, add texture and a human dimension when it comes to matters of profit. Rather than calling a charitable group or service center a "non-profit," Twist renames these vital strands in the human fabric "social-profit" organizations. As she says, "There is nothing 'non' about non-profits." There is a profit; it's called social profit. Similarly Kevin Danaher, founder of Global Exchange and the Green Festival uses the term "non-profit entrepreneur" to reflect the newly emerging philosophy in the world of philanthropy.

Nobel Peace Prize winner Dr. Mohammad Yunus, founder of the micro-lending movement, speaks of the rate of return in broader terms than money—focusing on the number of trees planted, lives saved, families salvaged, individuals educated, and villages lifted out of poverty. Dr. Yunus would like to see a "stock market" for social-profits that allows them to compete with each other, to check and compare their rate of "social" and "environmental" return, thus bringing the concept of competition in its real meaning to philanthropy.

> [Sidebar] Competition in its highest form is about competing to bring out the 'best' in each other, a feedback mechanism showing us where we have room for improvement and where we can congratulate ourselves for a job well done.

We are involved in a cultural evolution. Ours is an age of party-cipation. No longer are we limited to learning from gurus, teachers, and scripture. The Global Citizens who we are consciously evolving into have access to all traditions; they can pick and choose and custom-design their own unique spiritual practice and path. The spiritual hierarchy of love and support has spread and awakened consciousness throughout the species so that we are now able to mentor one another

In Silicon Valley, the influence of these Knights of E-Commerce has moved light years beyond the work of organized sects and brotherhoods. Rather, the work or ideals of Sacred Commerce now manifests worldwide, at the stroke of a key, every minute on every continent, spontaneously, through the individual work of many different people who will never meet.

In today's world, religious and esoteric orders are no longer needed to elevate the overall resonance of the culture. The work is carried forward through loosely affiliated groups of like-minded people who are connected through horizontal networks of equal relationships, rather than across the vertical chain of command typical of the traditional organizations of the past. These horizontal networks are spreading across every continent, across all genders and cultures, across all ages, classes, religions and beliefs throughout the Web. We're witnessing the rise of the Global Citizen.

Right use of technology is more crucial now than ever before. At this time in history our machines aspire to near-human capacities and reflect both our conscious and unconscious selves. We, as the gods of these machines, must now be clear on what manner of gods we wish to be, and on what kind of future we are intent on creating, for the machines will be sure to reflect that intent. Over the ages the Merchant Priests were directly or partially responsible for many of the creative enterprises that uplifted humanity and contributed to cultural evolution. Their efforts laid the foundation for a spreading global middle class, and spread the seeds of the capitalism that has bankrolled democracy and freedom for well over a billion people, first in the West and now spreading all over the world. Yet as "Priests," their historic business success remained deeply reflective of their continued commitment to self-realization.

This spiritual current we are speaking of today is transparent, all-inclusive and available to all. You need not take vows or wear a robe and collar to tap the pulse or be carried upstream by this gracious current. The Merchant Priesthood has passed the baton to the collective and infused the shared domain of human thought and aspiration with these ideas and values. The sacred dimension of commerce calls to us from the future, inviting us to party-cipate. The next important wake up call alerts us to exercise care and attention as we select the products and services we exchange. As global citizens with one eye scanning ahead toward our most elegant future, we shop and spend and click and send with our ear to the ground, listening for the pulsing magnetic, the "strange attractor" that has always called us forward and called out our best: **beauty, goodness, and truth**, heralding the birth of the Sacred Consumer. It is this refined context and precise focus that allows the magic and the miracles to flow into the various avenues and enterprises we choose.

> **[Sidebar]** The Sacred Consumer is not only conscious of what they consume and it's impact on their body and the environment, but also how it impacts their consciousness and the consciousness of others.

In our day and age we face challenges and opportunities like no other time in history. With the coming together of the global village and the growth of the global economy, the true gift of Sacred Commerce—conscious evolution—requires an understanding of Emotional Alchemy. The first two aspects of the gift were fulfilled to a degree by the Merchant Priesthood. Their mantle is now being passed onto those of us who take up the challenge and opportunity to stretch into the future in new and magical ways, as we will see in Part Three. This component of Emotional Intelligence requires us to think and feel in such a way as to stretch our minds and our spheres of influence far beyond those of the men and women who came before us, thus propelling us into a conscious global transformation.

Many of you reading this book already see yourselves as social inventors or engineers. You are the heralds, the people bringing meaning, ethics, emotion and caring into business, education and government institutions. We are revolutionizing the way business gets done, the way we interact with each other, and the way we think.

As the sacred and the feminine returns to our daily lives, commerce will reveal its ultimate gift; a powerful tool for conscious evolution.

The Merchant Priest is awakening in all of us. The ancients set the frame and crafted the morphic field; now we play our part in spinning out the meme (cultural information that propagates from one mind to another). **The secret is out: partycipation in the pursuit of beauty, goodness, and truth IS the**

blueprint for a new humanity. The time of tooth-and-claw struggle and martyrdom is over; the time for magic and miracles is now.

By reading this far, you have nearly completed the Merchant Priesthood initiation. What is left is for you to take the mantle. Vows of celibacy and poverty are not required. All that is required is a willingness to receive and a desire to party-cipate in manifesting the dream of prosperity, peace, and conscious evolution for all.

How are you PARTY-CIPATING?

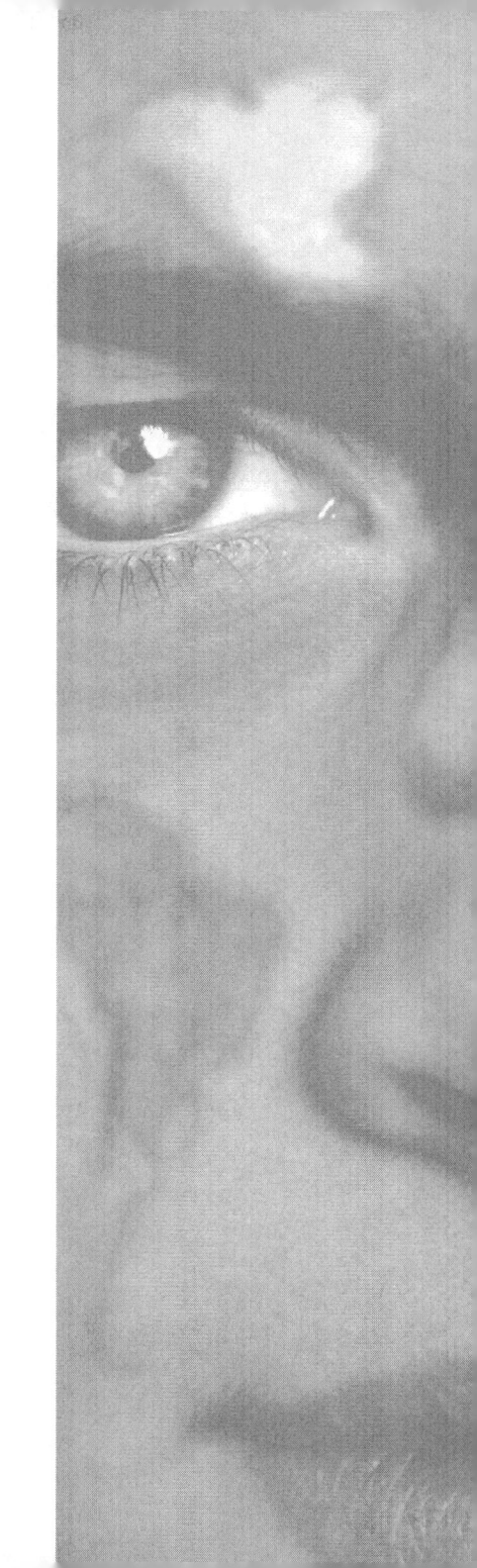

Part Three:
The Emotional Alchemist

Emotional Intelligence

The Merchant Priests' greatest skill and challenge was to be able to take their inner training into the marketplace instead of preserving it for the safe and serene environment of a monastery. It's one thing to be stabilized in radiant presence when protected by monastery walls, but quite another to be able to sustain the resonance of harmony and compassion when in the thick of daily transactions and emotions.

When a Merchant Priest or a modern day Knight of Commerce steps into the market place – whether it be a souk in old Cairo or a board meeting in Silicon Valley – they need to be sensitive to and aware of the swirl of emotional energies that are shaping and influencing their environment. Nothing can shake us from our center more easily than the numbers in our bank balance or the affairs of the heart.

In the market place both of these can be present at the same time. One person may be jealous of another; several may be absorbed in their greed; others will be speaking and acting from fear; while a couple of associates in the corner may be in the midst of some smoldering argument or in the beginnings of a passionate love affair. Other feelings – deceit, betrayal, mistrust, or fraud – may also be present.

The Merchant Priest will have trained long and hard to be able to step into that environment and not only be protected from all the forces swirling around him/her, but also be able to harmonize the energies of the group for the benefit of all and for the good of the transaction, whether it be the sale of a pound of apples or the merger of two Fortune 500 companies.

The Merchant Priests' secret power lies in Emotional Intelligence. This is what we need to learn today more urgently than ever. Psychology has helped us bring something of this skill into the arena of personal development and intimate relationships, and initiatives are under way to educate children in Emotional Literacy. But it is the Merchant Priest's task – and it is a formidable one – to infuse the work environment and corporate culture with this capacity to work intelligently with one's own emotions. This is what I set out to do in my first book, *Executive EQ Emotional Intelligence in Leadership and Organizations,* which I co-authored with Robert Cooper and which has helped executives and business leaders around the world to begin to build a sustainable a new corporate culture.

The Merchant Priesthood in ancient Egypt was trained to gain proficiency in not just one but all four levels of Emotional Intelligence. The first stage was to become literate in the language—to learn the alphabet and grammar of our emotions, so that we know what we are feeling when we are feeling it and are able to name and express that feeling to ourselves and to others as required. This is Emotional Literacy.

It's rather like a trainee chemist learning the table of elements. They learn that H is for hydrogen, He for helium, O for oxygen, and so on. Knowing the properties of these different gases enables the trainee to use the elements in combination to get the desired reaction in his test tube. In the same way, we must learn the effects of different emotions and their combinations, so as to avoid an explosion in the laboratory of the body-mind. To read our emotional chart in this way is to learn the relational world's primary language.

The Merchant Priest knew that strong feelings like anger, fear, and jealousy are not "wrong" or "bad." Far from it, they are perfectly appropriate in the right situation and have enabled the human race to survive. This is why they are hard wired into our nervous system. If we deny or ignore these messages from the lower part of the body, we waste the vital energy and information that they carry. It is better to recognize and harness these raw energies rather than letting them cause damage by spilling out of us unconsciously.

Emotional Literacy teaches us to respect these emotions that are broadcast from the "lower centers," the first three chakras in the human organism and to pay attention to them as valuable signals that are trying to tell us something about our relationship to our environment. In time we learn to see these emotions not so much as base in themselves but rather as denser expressions of the higher energies.

Woven into the very root of our being, in what the yogis call the first chakra at the base of the pelvis or as Maslow would call it the survival instinct, is the response that registers in consciousness as the fight or flight mechanism. The emotion that drives this response is fear, especially the mother of all other fears, the fear of death. The second chakra, situated behind the navel, governs our basic need for safety and security. Anger is the driving force here. Then the third chakra, in the solar plexus, just beneath the diaphragm, is the seat of our need for belonging and relationship. This is where jealousy thrives.

The Merchant Priests of ancient Egypt saw these emotions first and foremost as a source of energy, information and attraction. Our science tells us they are electro-magnetic energy. E-motions are "energy in motion," pure and simple. Just like electricity and magnetism, they are morally neutral. How we use electricity or our emotions, however, determines whether their effect is positive or negative. If we put our finger in an electric socket we will get a shock. If we direct that current by installing a bulb and switching on the light, we may find ourselves saying "Wow!" instead of "Ouch!" This is the way the Merchant Priests saw emotions. Some are constricting and some are expansive, but none are good or bad. The constricting emotions of anger, fear, and jealousy focus us and direct us into a certain path of action, while the expansive emotions of love, joy and beauty open us up to a higher degree of options and choices. Both are needed. Our emotions are raw energy that we can transform into power and use with efficiency and grace to bring more elegance into our daily life.

The Merchant Priests would welcome whatever emotion arose in them and engage it in dialogue. With the assistance of associated bodily sensations, they would 'feel' for the root cause of the emotion instead of taking it at its surface value. They would reflect upon it and look deeper to see its components and then dive as deeply as they could into the felt experience to unearth the real issues that the emotion was trying to bring to their attention. The more they were able to befriend their emotions, the more conscious their feeling self became and the easier it was to transmute the denser emotional frequencies into the finer.

They knew that anger, fear, or jealousy do not simply arise out of nowhere, for no reason, like some arbitrary or freak thunderstorm. They would receive those emotions as valuable messengers with information about their relationship with their current environment/reality. They would know that anger, for example, is a signal that things are not happening the way they want them to. They would receive it as a call to responsibility and would take action accordingly. Anger is a raw energy that wants and needs to be directed. If we fail to direct it consciously, we are liable to do damage.

Learning to harness anger and to direct it to positive ends was a highly refined art among the Egyptians. Just as the Eskimos have some thirty different words for snow and the Indians, who have made a science of the breath, have many names for the various breathing patterns, so too the Egyptians had twenty to thirty different names for each of the root emotions of fear, anger, and jealousy.

The Merchant Priest would harness these energies by bringing them first into conscious awareness. This is the foundation of Emotional Literacy – to pause when we are afraid and to notice: *my body is sending me a signal of fear.* To make the emotion conscious like this may sound simple, and in a way it is. But it takes an intentional moment of self awareness which can be easily drowned out by the power of the emotion's habitual tendency to trigger an unconscious knee-jerk of fight or flight.

The power and persuasiveness of the knee-jerk reaction is hardly surprising. After all, it has been programmed into us genetically for millions of years. It is in our biochemistry. But in our day-to-day reality we very rarely encounter situations that are truly life threatening. Even so, we all too easily succumb to our biochemistry and overreact, as if we were in fact in some mortal danger. The good news is that, more recently in our evolution, we have developed a neo-cortex that does enable us to bypass the automatic reaction with a conscious response that is more appropriate for the reality of the situation we find ourselves in.

It is not enough to know this theoretically, however. We need to see and acknowledge the power of our unconscious conditioning, to learn the steps toward conscious intervention, and then consistently put those steps into practice. Once we have trained ourselves to feel the emotion that is rising in us and to name it, we can exercise discernment and make an informed choice of response according to the situation.

Just as a pianist has first to learn the name and the difference between the various notes on his keyboard, so the Merchant Priest becomes literate in the types of emotion at his/her disposal and their uses. Then, as the pianist learns to gather the notes into a tune and eventually into a whole sonata, so the Merchant Priest develops the skill and dexterity in "playing" his/her emotions to maximum effect, creating beautiful realities for themselves and for the benefit of all. This is Emotional

Literacy, which includes a practical intuition that allows the Merchant Priest to just 'know' what the appropriate response is at any given time without the need for a process of conscious reasoning. Once literate the priests would go about exercising their skills and emotional muscles, to develop Emotional Fitness in the same way a good pianist exercises his musical skills by taking on a difficult piece. With Emotional Fitness we add the emotional component to the realms of character, integrity, trust, resilience, and relationships, and we strengthen and harness those qualities and give them depth. By so doing we move from developing life skills to gaining life mastery.

I remember the time Rowan came to me after meditating and said, "I just found out that I am a liar, and that I lack Character." She was obviously in a state of shock about this, as was I. As far as I knew she never lies and has high character. "What an earth do you mean?" I asked. She replied, "I may not lie about the facts and figures, and in fact have always prided myself on my honesty, but I just realized I lie about how I feel all the time, and this is far worse. My friends ask me 'How are you?' and I say 'Fine' even when I'm not. I am so scared of the impact of my feelings I just lie about them." As you can imagine this was a big realization for her. She realized she had a lot of room to strengthen her character. By adding the emotional component she added depth, allowing her to deal with a far wider range of experiences.

This leads to the third degree of Emotional Intelligence which we call Emotional Depth. This is where you meet your shadow self, slay your dragons, and find your treasures. In the depth of the pool of emotions, it requires a willingness to look both your light and dark shadows squarely in the eye and acknowledge them as yours, consciously choosing what you want to keep and what it is time to let go of. It is where you touch your sense of majesty, greatness and destiny—your unique talent and genius.

Now we are approaching the stage that might be compared to the soloist in a concert. The Merchant Priest who has reached this level acts from a core of fundamental integrity and authentic presence. When they act they do so from an inner stillness, even though they may be outwardly engaged in anger or other powerful emotion. If s/he displays anger, s/he does so consciously in order to create a specific effect. They are fully committed to the greater good and act accordingly, whatever the situation may require. This is the root of their authority that those around them can feel as soon as he or she enters a room. Imagine the difference it would make in our world if CEO's were able to lead their organizations from this place of stability and emotional mastery in themselves!

This is the urgent task before us today. But the good news is that what took a Merchant Priest twenty years to master in Ancient Egypt can be learned today in far less time, with all the support, e-technology, and the global context we enjoy today. By mastering the realm of feelings with the proper use of Emotional Intelligence, we can have access to huge reserves of previously untapped power that can give us constant feedback and guide us toward ever greater profitability and success in the arena of not just one but of all four bottom lines—profitability, employee welfare, environmental impact, and self-realization.

Nowhere is this more possible than in the still largely unexplored territory of the World Wide Web, one of the most exciting and remarkable human adventures of all time. Month by month, year by year, the Web is taking us into new territories and possibilities that we never even dreamed of a year earlier. The Knights of E-Commerce are the new cutting edge of human culture, just as the Knights Templar were in another earlier seminal period of history. It offers a remarkable opportunity to blend our material goals with our spiritual ones, to become truly global citizens, and to extend our compassion and empathy across the planet in everything we do.

This level of attainment is an indication that we have reached the fourth and final level of Emotional Intelligence, which we call Emotional Alchemy. Here we are on the accelerated slope; we achieve a rarefied state of intuitive flow and self mastery. We begin to actively or consciously create the future.

Emotional Alchemy

When *Executive EQ* was first published we wondered if a phrase like "Emotional Alchemy" would land like a foreign tongue on the ears of a corporate world where reason was the primary language. In the early 90's alchemy of any kind was too far-fetched for some and too esoteric for others. We knew that including such a concept was a risk; nonetheless, we followed our intuition and went with it. A decade has passed since *Executive EQ* was first published and its success has validated the wisdom of that risk.

How little we knew about Emotional Alchemy then! It took me and Rowan another ten years of inner exploration, practicing EQ, and the discovery of quantum physics till we finally got it and are able to experience it and begin to articulate it.

The word alchemy comes from the Arabic, *al chimia*, which in the early Middle Ages simply meant 'chemistry.' The budding science of chemistry and a growing interest in the material world and its material formation was introduced into Europe through the Muslim Moors who ruled southern Spain in the Middle Ages. The cities of Granada and Cordoba were Europe's greatest centers of civilization in the 11th and 12th centuries, and they attracted scholars, mystics, and merchants of all three religious persuasions – Jewish, Muslim, and Christian. These cities were themselves a sort of alchemical retort in which different strands of esoteric knowledge were combined to create fresh and visionary insights into the potential of human nature.

Until that time, Western civilization had been entirely absorbed in the Christian story, and the culture as a whole had eyes only for spiritual realities and the afterlife. The material world was considered a vale of tears, something to pass through as quickly as possible in order to reach the 'real' life which lay beyond death. But in southern Spain at this time, new interests and new ways of thinking began to take root which gave value to the world of matter as well as the world of spirit. It was in this atmosphere that the interest in chemistry and the sciences of matter began to grow.

And it was there, too, that alchemy as we use the word today began to emerge – a study of how it might be possible to refine the material energies in the human being to the point where they miraculously transform into spiritual energies. Far from trying to escape the body and its denser energies for some rarified spiritual realm, these explorers saw the material world and the human body as the raw material for their own spiritual transformation.

While there were certainly many who took this transformative ideal only in a literal sense of the quest to turn a base metal like lead into pure gold, the true alchemists saw their own human body and mind as the real spiritual laboratory. For them the raw material of their experiments was their emotions. They sought to transmute the constricting emotions of anger, fear and jealousy into passion, compassion, and empathy and in that way, ultimately, to unite in the human body and on this earth with the God/Goddess that is All.

The Emotional Alchemist understands the basic tenets of chemistry and applies them to the emotional realm. The chemical reaction that occurs when two hydrogen atoms combine with one oxygen atom to make water is well understood by any student of high school chemistry. What is not so well understood is that a similar natural reaction occurs in our biochemistry. The Merchant Priests understood this and used their knowledge to influence and leverage human emotion. They could turn anger into courage by applying a specific alchemical operation. Far more than a strategy to manage or manipulate emotions, this alchemical treatment is actually an invocation that creates magic. The treatment is so simple and elegant that anyone can test it out and put it to good use right away. There are many levels and nuances of Emotional Alchemy, and like anything it is a skill that can be continuously refined over a lifetime. However, there is one 'pocket remedy' that we will share with you here that anyone can use to transform a situation in an instant. The Merchant Priests called this basic operation "add a drop of joy."

Here's how it works. Let's say you feel angry. Webster's dictionary defines anger from 'a feeling of extreme annoyance, all the way to passion.' Every emotion has a specific chemical signature; we call this biochemistry. Your brain and your endocrine glands secrete distinct hormones with every emotional state. What is important to remember is that emotions are electro-magnetic energies. A flash of anger is a spray of hormonal drops that corresponds to the feeling we call 'mad.' Anger alone is just as likely to provoke an act of courage as an act of impulsive retaliation or an attack that you will later regret.

What the Merchant Priests of old Egypt understood — and this is key — is really quite elegant and simple: They understood the value of joy in refining and transmuting emotions. By adding a drop of joy to anger, an alchemical reaction occurs. Anger turns into courage.

How do we add a drop of joy? The best way is to feel it, which is easy when we are emotionally literate and fit. *We can also learn to conjure joy at will by calling on the memory of joy.* Consider this: your brain does not know the difference between an event that is actually occurring in the moment and an event that is occurring in your imagination. When you remember and relive a joyful moment, your body will create the chemistry of that experience. This can work to your advantage. One of my favorite ways of conjuring joy is bringing to mind the day our publisher for *Executive EQ* offered us an unusually large offer for a business book. I remember jumping up and down on my bed in sheer joy.

The extreme delight of that moment readily returns to my body and mind every time I conjure joy by calling up that memory. When I return to the matter at hand, the joy I have conjured sprinkles its biochemical hormonal 'juice' over the situation. Not only has my biochemistry and perspective changed, but my options for handling the situation became more varied and expansive.

It's important to note here the difference between joy and happiness. Happiness arises when you satisfy your needs, which Maslow lists as a hierarchy going all the way from survival through security, relationship, self-esteem, all the way to beauty. The meeting of each of these needs creates happiness. Joy on the other hand occurs when you meet your preferences. Preferences are things we like or enjoy to do vs. what we need to do. Watching TV, going to a rock concert, or having sex are preferences. Something we like to do. For example, the big advance for my book did not meet the needs of survival, security, or belonging. It did, however, line up with my preferences which were to have impact and share Emotional Intelligence with as many people as possible. I liked the idea of having the book out there. It gave me self esteem and lifted me into a state of joy.

The Hierarchy of Needs

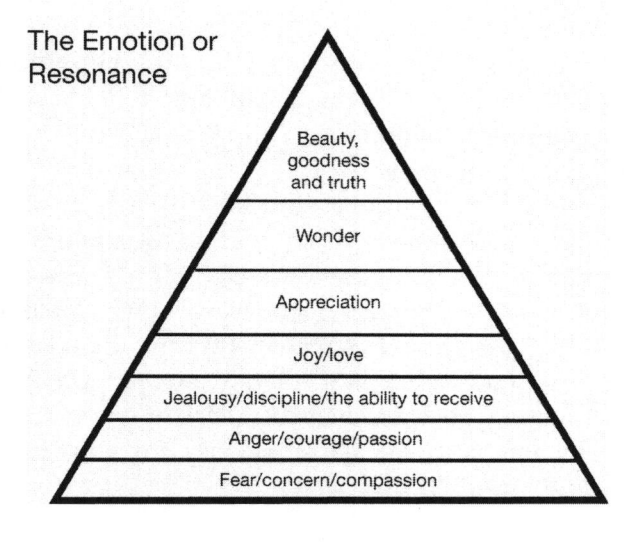

- Spirituality/self-realization/aesthetics
- Vision, knowing, understanding
- The expression of creativity/productivity
- Esteem/loving relationships
- Community/belonging
- Safety/security
- Survival

The Emotion or Resonance

- Beauty, goodness and truth
- Wonder
- Appreciation
- Joy/love
- Jealousy/discipline/the ability to receive
- Anger/courage/passion
- Fear/concern/compassion

Fear is a signal that something in your world needs attention. When there is cause for concern there is a fear response in the body. Seen in this light, fear is a positive emotion, one that can guide you to act with wisdom on behalf of the people, places and things you care most about. Imagine for a moment that your college-bound son decides he wants to cut down on his fossil fuel use by riding a motorcycle instead of driving his gas-guzzling pick-up truck. You are afraid for him, and that fear has kept you from sleeping well for several nights and has been at the root of many arguments.

So you add a drop of joy to your fear by remembering the day he burst through the front door and told you he had won the school election and was now president of his senior class. Your body responds by adding the chemistry of that joy to the chemistry of fear about his buying that Yamaha. This allows your mind to let go of the urge to control your son; instead, your mind becomes more spacious. The fear moves to concern. You also feel compassion and even admire his attempt to make an environmentally conscious choice. With this biochemical boost you can see the situation from an expanded viewpoint. A broader outlook at the situation makes it easier to problem-solve in a creative spirit. You ask your son to look into a motorcycle safety course and go shopping with him to choose the best helmet and protective clothing. Your fear reaction alone would not allow for this opening.

We can transmute jealousy and lift it to a higher octave. At the most basic level jealousy is an issue of ownership. The green monster appears when a question arises: *Is this mine or not? Will the love I cherish be taken away?* If yes, we get busy defending what is ours. In the best-case scenario we become the champion and claim what is ours with honor, dignity, and respect for all concerned. Anyone who has achieved sufficient emotional maturity and enlightenment to recognize jealousy for what it is knows better than to let it spiral down into envy or rage. Instead, we talk to the green monster and reason with him. If we determine that what we feel jealous over is not ours, the next step becomes obvious. We let go, holding what we want in our heart and ask to receive what is truly ours. One drop of joy added to jealousy becomes discipline. One drop of joy over discipline becomes the ability to receive what's truly ours.

Mastery at this level gives one unique powers. This is not self control or mind control or any kind of control. This is alchemy of the highest order. Like the alchemists who turned base metal into gold, the Merchant Priests learned to turn constricting emotions into the golden opportunity that is passion, compassion and empathy. Understanding emotions as a source of energy and information, the Emotional Alchemist can lift that energy to a higher octave.

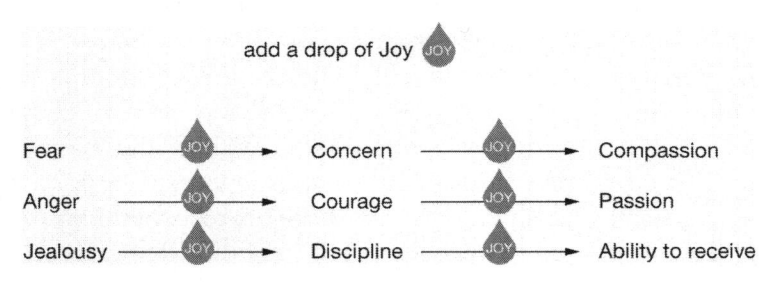

add a drop of Joy

Fear	→	Concern	→	Compassion
Anger	→	Courage	→	Passion
Jealousy	→	Discipline	→	Ability to receive

Sometimes, when I am at the last stages of completing a project, I run out of the passion needed to finish it. The clock is ticking, so I sit down in meditation and feel the anger related to the situation for a minute or so until enough anger hormones are released into my body/mind. Then I conjure a memory of joy and allow the joy 'juices' to mix up with the anger, resulting in a sense of courage and passion rising in my body and mind, giving me the fuel that is needed to finish my project.

Now let's look at what happens to someone who gets into intense jealousy while they are in a state of extreme anger and don't have the tools to process, express and transform that anger and jealousy consciously. The alchemical reactions of the anger and jealousy juices mixing create a resonance from which revenge or rage can precipitate.

Learn to transmute emotions with a drop of joy and you place yourself in a position of power. The secret of Emotional Alchemy is not limited to the drop of joy technique. The second great secret of the Emotional Alchemist is understanding the magic of resonance. S/he knows that by changing the resonance they change the reality.

More and more the existence of subtle energies and their responsiveness to our thoughts is being verified by experiments in quantum physics. Concepts like resonance are no longer the exclusive language of metaphysicians, nor can they be dismissed as 'new age' drivel.

Today the secrets of alchemy are in the public domain and we can speak of these matters freely. Documentary films such as *What The Bleep Do We Know?* and Rhonda Byrne's film *The Secret* have brought quantum physics into the living rooms of mainstream viewers. In the weeks after Oprah Winfrey did two hour-long shows featuring Rhonda Byrne and other experts from her film, we heard grammar school kids begin to experiment with this new view of reality and talk about what might be accomplished using The Secret.

To further understand the notion of resonance, let's review a few basic concepts from quantum physics. The main premise of quantum physics reveals that particles—blips of light, frequencies and vibrations—are everywhere. When they come together, they create a synergy, a standing wave or resonance far stronger than the sum of its parts. Take love, for example—it's a resonance. Inside love there are many particles, such as trust, giving, intimacy, caring, safety, nurturing, and knowing. All these frequencies come together as particles to create the resonance or standing wave we call love. Whatever is observed, the equivalent reality manifests. As quantum physicists say, the resonance or standing wave collapses and becomes a reality.

Scientific breakthroughs that vastly expand our understanding of the universe bring with them a whole new view of how reality functions. Notions such as "you create your own reality 100%" and "the law of attraction" that once may have been suspect and readily dismissed as so much metaphysical mumbo-jumbo can now be verified by leading edge science. Ideas like alchemy can now be brought out of the shadow lands of the arcane and into the realm of the good, the true (scientifically verifiable), and the beautiful.

All this is moving us toward an energy perspective, more oriented toward drawing in our future than concerning ourselves with the past. Western psychology asserts that the memory of a past event lives on in the present and can determine the quality of our everyday experience today. This is a dimension of reality governed by the law of cause and effect. Of course it is a valid perspective, but it is not the entire picture. In another perspective on reality, one can use the concept of the future as a means to determine a present reality against the backdrop of the past.

For example, it is possible to visualize and attune to the highest possibility that our future may hold and begin to "resonate" with that possibility, attracting it to the present. When we learn to hold an optimistic vibration of grand possibilities of the future in this way, we are actually drawing our future toward us by living out the vision and frequency we hold of it in the present. In this way, *the effect becomes the cause. This is the magnetism or law of attraction.*

Another way the law of attraction works is in the area of health. When we have constricting emotions left unattended they tend to come together as a resonance or a synergy stronger than the sum of all its part to create a receptacle or attractor for certain viruses or even accidents to come our way. We have inadvertently created the perfect Petri dish/resonance to attract that particular malady. Healing happens when one or more of the components of the resonance is eliminated or cancelled, thus robbing the illness of its environment and allowing a different resonance to form and a different reality to manifest. Working this way the healings are often magical. When looked at like this illness is far quicker to heal. When we change the mental/emotional soup (resonance) we create a new reality.

Our experience of love will be colored by the lens through which we observe it - by the particular group of particles that make up the standing wave that we call love. If my resonance of love includes the ingredient "love hurts" (because that was my experience growing up) or if love to me includes being humiliated, then when that love resonance "collapses" into my reality, it will have that flavor. My resonance of love I create will be made up of my unique list of ingredients. My ingredients – my thoughts (conscious, semi-conscious, and unconscious), feelings, beliefs, attitudes, choices, and decisions about love – all exist as frequencies of vibration coming together. One negates the other, one adds to another, one combines with another to become a resonance. We still cannot see it at this stage. Once the wave collapses into reality, I find myself in a love affair that has my precise list of ingredients in my love-stew – my personalized signature.

So how do we change our resonance to create magic? We look at all the various constituents that make up our particular resonance of love, for example, and then we make a commitment to work on deleting those aspects that prevent the resonance from being the highest it can be. If, say, we have developed a habit of associating love with pain or betrayal, we work to change our thought and belief system and heal our emotions so that our resonance is free of those limiting perspectives. We consciously process our beliefs to the point where our resonance is one of success.

Lastly, let's look at what can happen when you are working with another who shares an understanding of resonance. Rowan and I call this practice "holding the resonance"—it is the cornerstone and primary vow of our relationship. When either of us feels down or is in a low resonance for some reason—be it tiredness, illness, stress or any of life's ever-arising challenges—the other takes a stand and holds the resonance. With pairs or groups of people, when one person is down the other(s) tend to go down to meet him or her. Too often this results in two or more being down and getting stuck. A clear way to avert this pattern becomes obvious when we look at the dynamic from an energetic perspective. Keep in mind what we know about resonance. When two frequencies meet, one of three things happen—the lower one comes up, the higher goes down or they meet in the middle. In the context of our relationship the "better off" of the two of us always "holds the resonance." Said another way, rather than crawl down into the other's pit we lower a ladder.

Perhaps the best example of this can be seen in the case of a woman named Shelley Yates whose son nearly drowned after her car hydroplaned off the road and sank to the bottom of a flooded marsh. When the boy was brought to the hospital, doctors declared him brain dead with non-viable organs and 1% chance of survival. The boy's mother, having just had a near death experience herself in the same accident, was in a kind of altered state, with heightened awareness and sensitivity. She knew if she could hold the resonance high enough in the room that it could save his life. She rallied everyone she knew to hold a vigil at his bedside. One person at a time, for twenty minutes each, those people shared their energy field with the boy, holding a healing intent. The mother instructed the doctors not to talk about any of the possible negative outcomes in her son's presence, rather to talk to her in the hall. Seventy-two hours later he opened his eyes and recognized his mother. Today even his lingering memory problems have healed.

This example introduces us to the ways in which Emotional Intelligence can act as the precursor to spiritual intelligence. When we have developed the neural circuitry of an Emotional Alchemist, a true relationship of partnership with the Divine becomes possible and, once established, gives us the unique ability to co-create reality. We cease to operate within a "cause and effect" perspective and begin to "create" by resonating with magical and elegant future realities that we *choose* to attract. In this way, as we said earlier, *the effect becomes the cause*. When we begin to operate with the intention of creating positive realities for ourselves *as well as for all those within our sphere of influence*, the balance of power shifts in our favor as universal forces coalesce and realign to support our intent. We become aligned to what we call "The Pulse," which is the subject of the next chapter.

Partnership with the Pulse

Although a relationship with the Pulse is available for all people at all times, a relationship of partnership can only really be achieved once a certain level of Emotional Intelligence has been mastered.

While emotions and the associated matrix of psychological forces are an essential foundation of our existence, we humans are also spiritual beings. Today's Knights of Commerce have a personal relationship with the Divine – that ultimate resonant energy of the universe we call "The Pulse." We leave behind the childlike relationship to God that pleads *Help me with this, God. Will you do it for me, please? Please might I have a miracle?* We are no longer in servitude to the Powers That Be; we enter a partnership relationship. We come well-versed in the language of relationship; we come equipped with our passion, compassion, and our ability to receive. We know how to transmute energy with joy and create magic with Emotional Alchemy.

When this core relationship with the Pulse has been established, true miracles can actually happen. To establish that partnership with the Pulse, we use the fuel of our passion and enthusiasm, and the skill of generating the correct resonance, as we discussed in the previous chapter. Passion is the modem that connects us to the entire Web of Creation. It is the force for the good and the true that enables our sense of interconnectedness and joy. The Greek root of the word 'enthusiasm' means being filled or infused with the breath of a god. This is why the quality of enthusiasm has always been so highly prized. Enthusiasm is a natural expression of the individual soul, a hint of the divinity bestowed on each of us as our potential for happiness.

In its higher octaves enthusiasm turns to joy. Joy is the spontaneous expression of the human spirit. The more fully we engage in our lives and dive into our days without resistance, the more our joy will burst forth and infect everyone around with delight for our common purpose, whatever it may be. The more joy we have in our life, the more we know that our life is not ours alone, but rather that joy is a co-creation with its own inherent purpose and spirit.

The access point for the Pulse is the human heart. The heart is like a tuning fork with the ability to sense the particular spectrum of this energy of existence. This energy – the Pulse – resonates across a graduated spectrum of forces, all the way up to the Infinite Source known by any of a thousand names for God. As such, the highest wisdom is available to those with the ability to tune into this Pulse. The quality and quantity of wisdom available exists in proportion to our sensitivity to the Pulse and our degree of attunement.

Our ability to attune to the Pulse is also directly related to the level of commitment we bring to this matter of *self responsebility*. Most of us have spent years engaging in personal growth and conscious evolution, and recognize this level of self responsibility. We don't blame or point fingers if we find an ingredient in our love relationship that we do not like. We get busy unearthing our core beliefs and attitudes and making the change at that level. If we have been diligent in our personal evolution, we may even be in the stage a Merchant Priest reached later in life where the root emotions (fear, anger and jealousy) automatically transmute into higher frequencies because they occur in the ocean of joy.

Everything that exists emanates a spectrum of frequencies which, taken together, form a particular energy signature, note, or resonance. As the person becomes sensitive to his or her particular resonance, s/he can begin to consciously act in tune with this note.

As I explored my own resonance and became more conscious of its different components, I found the expansive frequencies of love, courage, curiosity, enthusiasm, joy, fun and the willingness to have impact, along side the more constricting frequencies of needing to be in control, perfection, arrogance and judgment, all mixing together to create the person I am. In my own personal evolution, as I consciously take out and heal the constricting emotions and add to my resonance frequencies that balance me—peace, stillness, and humility— a whole new resonance is shaped, an alchemical reaction or a metamorphosis happens, and a more beautiful me is created. This is something I do again and again. Constricting emotions do not go away. When I am under stress, they raise their heads again, and each and every time I am the one with the choice to listen to them or to raise my resonance again.

The Pulse has certain qualities – beauty, goodness, and truth are primary among them – and as we cultivate these qualities we learn how to develop and then project the resonance of the Pulse in our everyday life. Not only this, but the Pulse contains the blueprint of our possible future and destiny. As we bring the Pulse's unique resonance into our daily existence, we literally draw our future to us in the here and now.

To do this is to enter the realm of miracles. Magic is a shift in perspective that allows us to see what wasn't there a moment ago. Any magician knows the importance of *perspective* to his craft, for it is perspective that lends magic to every sleight of hand. When we make magic by changing the resonance consciously, for example, we apply a sort of inner sleight of hand to our current reality. This is the magic that opens the window to unseen possibilities. This is how magic can shift your reality.

Miracles are of another order altogether, and that is where a relationship with the Pulse is essential. Miracles are events or phenomena that happen without effort, and that turn out better than we could ever desire, expect, or imagine. It is the result of co-creating with the divine. They typically startle us because they seem to come out of nowhere.

Through co-creation with the Pulse a synergy is generated that gives results far larger than the sum of its parts, though this can only happen if we come to the partnership emotionally clear. There are only two rules that come with this co creation. First, our success is always shared in acknowledgment of the part played by our greater partner. Second, if for any reason our venture does not live up to expectations, then we must take full responsibility for any failure ourselves. The beauty of the path of Sacred Commerce is that the unexpected is a constant companion, and you begin to live with the awareness that anything can happen when you are partnered with the Pulse.

Imagine for a moment the enormous benefit of a working partnership with God. You might compare it to suddenly teaming up with a high level business partner who immediately and effortlessly affords you access to unforeseen resources and an impressive list of contacts. To enter this realm of miracles, you must align yourself to the resonance of the transcendent qualities – beauty, truth, goodness, ecstasy, and always, love. Then, as miracle after miracle unfolds before your eyes, you realize that clearly the gods are present and at play in your reality. You feel the divine presence permeate your reality. The presence of the miraculous then lifts you to a whole new level of gratitude and appreciation. One of the qualities of appreciation is seeing the wonder in people and things everywhere. At this point base emotions can automatically be transmuted in the ocean of joy in which you abide.

The task of the Emotional Alchemist is to ally themselves with the Pulse as s/he works to manage and co-create the world with this unique support. As a source of energy, insight and inspiration the Pulse is second to none. As one forms an inner bond with this power via reflection, meditation, and visualization, a variety of beneficial qualities naturally arises. To realize this alliance the individual must come to co-exist with a level of consciousness higher than the conscious ego. This perspective then becomes the foundation for all external alliances. Only with higher consciousness can our work be in service to something greater than ourselves.

This is what the Merchant Priests in ancient Egypt were trained to do. After their training, they went out into the world in service to their communities and humanity at large, while maintaining a partnership with the Pulse. A sense of elegance, ease and excellence accompanied their movements within society; there was no trace of the attitude of martyrhood that we see in many of the service and helping professions through out history and today. During periods when they ascended to prominence, they were the most revered class of priests, not unlike our honored Ph.D's. Through participation – the literal partnering with the Pulse – they made a project of lifting humanity out of poverty into abundance and peace. This unique partnership allowed them to conduct their affairs in the zone of the miraculous. They were awake and full of wonder at the majesty of existence beyond what even expectation and imagination might lead one to believe.

Emotional Alchemy alone is a phenomenal resource; but when combined with a direct relationship with the Pulse, the tectonic plates of your reality will begin to shift. If our experience – as well as that of close friends who have taken up the path – is any indication, you are in for a thrilling ride wherein *life becomes art*. Like the Merchant Priests of old, today's knights of commerce are thrilled by the work they do and the lives they lead. The more enthusiastic they are, and the more *they feel intensely with clear intent*, the more they turn any opportunity into a positive reality. And the more they attune to the Pulse, the more they are filled with appreciation and wonder, which are qualities we shall explore in the next chapter.

Appreciation and Wonder: Gateway to Beauty

Imagine what it is like to strike an unexpected business deal or come up with an innovation that will benefit hundreds of thousands of people. A woman might call a meeting between opposing parties in a hostile takeover situation and finesse a solution that rallies all involved around an unexpected collaboration that brings out each person's unique strength. When we tap into the Zone and reach a higher order or new synthesis in business we have that Midas touch that turns dross into gold. We know in these moments that the success is not ours alone. To touch this level is simultaneously humbling and exhilarating. We feel a profound gratitude for what we have had the deep pleasure and honor to co-create as it washes over us. The more this happens the more we feel a deep appreciation that adds value to everything we create, touch, or do. .

When we are in the zone in this way — whether it be the athlete moving beyond his former limitations to new heights of performance or the musicians in a band where suddenly everything falls into place and the music seems heaven sent; or when a quarterback receives the perfect pass and takes it into the end zone — whatever the context, in those moments we are one with the Pulse, and the resulting feeling state is gratitude and appreciation. The crowds shower the athlete or the musicians with their appreciation, and the individual feels profoundly grateful.

To feel grateful is to be full of greatness. In a moment of gratitude we become greater and more valuable than who we are in a personal sense. We are the living breathing frequency of appreciation. Everything we see or touch increases in value. Our house or our land appreciates when we feel grateful and honored by it, and we in turn bless it with our gratitude and care.

Gratitude is the awareness and acknowledgment that life is far bigger than my individual self—that I exist in every moment by virtue of forces far beyond my understanding. Gratitude is the ability to notice the wonder of life in the great moments as well as the small ones. The most seemingly insignificant detail – a chance phone call, an unexpected opportunity, the door that opened when we thought it might close – all bring forward deep gratitude.

Everything that enters our life has its own place even if we don't know right away what that place is. Gratitude generates a flow of energy and warmth from each of us to everyone and everything for which we are thankful and appreciative, allowing genuine communication and heartfelt connection. Gratitude also keeps us in the benevolent care of humility and is the key to our ability to receive.

Once we become adept at creating magical realities and miracles in our life consciously, we can rest in a state of continual appreciation and wonder. This engages your soul and spirit in a whole new way and stirs up a special kind of allure that activates all your centers as you become something more than you were before. Some people begin to feel the Pulse quite strongly as the fourth chakra of the heart attunes to its frequency of love, enthusiasm and joy. The fifth chakra of the throat also responds, as if our voice were a string instrument crying out to be tuned. As the throat center is attuned, the voice gives expression to appreciation and gratitude, further extending the resonance we feel through the heart. The more we co-create with the Pulse the more appreciation we feel for the world around us and everything in it and the more we enter the WOW, a child-like state of open-eyed wonder. All our senses light up and we see the world in a grain of sand, as William Blake said. Hold a piece of wood in your hand and allow yourself to be absorbed in its texture, its density, the way it fits into your palm like a pebble. Let the feel of it, the look of it, and the smell of it erase all other thoughts in your mind. In this same wonder-filled way you might begin to hear your colleague's voice with a spontaneous attention that enables you to feel the tone of her deepest loves and longings – even though she may simply be asking you to pass a pencil.

Now you are living in the field of wonder. You smell the rain as you step out of the door in the morning and it stops you in your tracks. There, in the pouring of winter, in the middle of downtown, you stop and breathe in the glorious scent of the mountain air. You begin to really taste the food that you eat every morning, pausing between mouthfuls, and suddenly you notice the plethora of tastes that have just hit your palate. You revel in the tingling, the warmth, the savor of it all. Remember the saying "Come to god as a child, filled with that primal innocence and humility." This gateway invites us to be born again, induced by wonder in big and small ways every day. That sense of wonder is the womb where Beauty is conceived.

Beauty, Goodness, and Truth: The Eternal Verities

When your life is full of joy, appreciation, and wonder, the beauty of the world falls open before you like a book. The reality of the world, as the manifestation of the Pulse, is none other than Beauty, Truth and Goodness, which have been known throughout history as the "Eternal Verities." This is who we are; this is what everything is; there is only this.

This is the ultimate realization and the path of the Merchant Priesthood, past and present. It first burst into my own awareness in 1998 when I was meditating along with 300 other people at an event at the Holiday Inn at Los Angeles International Airport. The point of the meditation was to experience the birth of the universe first hand. Science tells us that with the big bang the universe was born. Subatomic particles emanating from this cosmic explosion filled the vast reach of space, becoming neutrons, protons, photons, then atoms and molecules, until these formations of early matter evolved into rocks and vegetables and animals – and eventually, humans.

In my vision that day, which has never left me, I experienced a romantic version of the big bang. The Goddess in all her glory seduced god and the two "made love" and Bang! The ecstasy generated by this glorious union seeded the universe with infinite units of consciousness from which I was/am one. As the universe was born, every molecule and atom carried the masculine fire or vital energy that we know as light and each atom and molecule also carried the essence of the goddess. Deep in meditation, the "Goddess" revealed herself to me as the quintessential expression of Beauty, Goodness, and Truth. That "first essence" registered on my awareness as the most exquisite and gentle vibration imaginable, pulsing in the core of my being and throbbing throughout my entire body.

Realizing that this is what gave birth to all function and form, I accepted Beauty, Goodness, and Truth as our true nature or essence. This indivisible trinity is what we are! Everybody and everything is beautiful, good, and true in essence! This is what scripture points to with expressions like "You are made in the image and likeness of God."

I was left with the exquisite resonance of "knowingness without certainty," often referred to as faith. I realized that our spiritual journey is to remember the truth of who we are, experiencing the goodness of our actions and becoming the Beautiful. Our purpose, then, can be seen as a "holy opportunity" to realize and express that trinity that is both our heritage and our birthright. Although the setting in a busy airport hotel in Los Angeles was a far cry from the "mountain top," I did have the sense that I had glimpsed the eternal. From then on this divine triad became driving forces that began to guide my life.

Philosophers and sages have known this the world over for thousands of years. Socrates was the first person in the West to name these eternal verities, but they are to be found at the heart of every great religious tradition East and West. Even the most hard core atheist would agree with them. In Father Thomas Dowd's blog he eloquently relates how they are harmonized with the three great Christian virtues Faith, Hope, and Love.

Faith is the virtue connected to Truth, and the human receptor for it is the mind/reason. Faith is not merely blind belief, but rather a choice to trust. We look for truth, often testing it first, but the more we see that it actually is true the more we trust it, until the choice to trust becomes almost automatic. Faith in God works like that. It is the knowingness with uncertainty that God exists. Our approach to God involves a genuine seeking for *truth about God*. Faith grows as our quest for the ultimate Truth continues, developing into a spontaneous habit of trust in God – the basis of a true relationship and partnership.

Hope is the virtue connected to Beauty, and for this the human receptor is the imagination. Hope rides on the wings of Beauty because of Beauty's capacity to lift us out of whatever situation we are in with an experience of ecstasy, or *ek-stasis*, the original Greek term which literally means "to be beside yourself." Isn't that what Beauty does? In the presence of something truly beautiful, we might gasp, whistle, clap, or simply admire. Time itself sometimes seems to stop as we are drawn into contemplation, the rest of the world falling away. Ordinary life is all too often filled with useless distractions and sufferings, but it all blows away like mist when Beauty shows up and puts us back in touch with the true meaning of our humanity. Hope is vibrant with positive expectation and anticipation and the echo that remains when the experience of ecstasy has passed.

This brings us to the greatest virtue of all, which is Love. Love is connected to Goodness, and conscience is the receptor that allows us to experience it. The philosophical category of the Good is broad indeed, but for our purposes it is simplest to focus on one small aspect, namely moral goodness. Simply put, there is a general human preference to be associated with good people rather than evil ones, and even when we do freely associate with evil people it is because we see some good in them that we want to be part of or possibly encourage.

Being around evil people raises tension, and being subject to evil acts and choices breeds hatred. On the other hand, being in the presence of moral goodness is profoundly satisfying and even rewarding when we choose to become agents of goodness. Love, in the end, is a desire to work for the good of others, but in so doing we discover that we are also achieving something Good for ourselves as well. Love becomes its own reward.

A quest for Truth, Beauty, and Goodness, then, is ultimately a search for a way of life rooted in Faith, Hope, and Love. And the more we become intimate with one of these great verities, the more we become aware of the presence of the other two. For as the poet John Keats said in his poem *Ode to a Grecian Urn*, "*Beauty is truth,* **truth is beauty** — *that is all ye know on earth, and all ye need to know.*"

Each of the three eternal verities is a resonance. Beauty, for example, is the resonance that can instantly lift you out of the ordinary world to a level of transcendence that immediately dissolves whatever problem might be present in your reality. In the presence of Beauty you don't need to go through the steps of transmuting anger to courage, to passion, to this and that. Anger just vanishes as if it were never there in the first place. Let's say you get in a disagreement with your mother. You walk out of the house angry as heck and slam the door. You drive off and see that the sun has begun to set. You stop to watch the gorgeous pink, crimson, and flaming orange colors splash across the sky. In an instant you transcend your angry feelings and get a glimpse of your mother's point of view. Passion fills your heart as you stand in awe of life's beauty splashing across the sky and filling your filial heart.

Beauty as defined by our friend Lazaris is comprised of eight distinct frequencies. When these frequencies come together, the resonance that is Beauty is formed. The first two frequencies are joy and peace. Usually these two are not felt together at the same time. Joy is masculine and very active; peace is feminine and passive. They would seem to cancel each other out. But in a state of beauty, looking at the sunset, you experience joy and peace simultaneously. Only rarely when we are in a state of beauty or ecstasy do joy and peace coincide. The same is true for serenity and exhilaration, and the other frequencies of Beauty — majesty and wonder, enchantment and inspiration. These pairs are masculine and feminine, and in Beauty they come together in synergy. When all eight frequencies combine, they create something beyond any of their individual qualities—they create Beauty.

In the realm of Beauty, everything is transcended. The portal to the miraculous opens. You move with excellence and elegance. With the least amount of energy spent, you get the maximum result. Through intentional focus we can learn to harness ecstasy and beauty as a way to transcend the past. Mystics and seers across the globe agree: the new world is not an improved version of what we have now. We are moving beyond. Through conscious evolution we transcend cause and effect. We learn in a whole new way and, with respect to our emotions, we learn to create states of enlightenment intentionally.

Our primary motivation ceases to be selfish; what we want most is to create Beauty. Beauty is not a collection of beautiful objects or even dazzling sunsets; beauty is a transcendent and functional energy in which we begin to evolve a new way of being. We know we have the option to make a conscious choice in any moment and orient around the eight frequencies of Beauty. The highest aspiration on the path of Sacred Commerce – as it was for the Merchant Priests – is to see the beautiful in everything and everyone, to always create the beautiful and to become more and more beautiful every day. As Rowan would tell you, she sees me as 75% beautiful, embodying six of the eight frequencies that make up beauty. Meaning when she is in my presence she might feel Joy, Exhilaration, Enchantment, Inspiration, the sense of Majesty and Wonder, but she does not necessarily feel Peace or Serenity (that magic of stillness), which shows me exactly what I need to work on, on my path to becoming more beautiful and resonating more strongly with the divine.

How Beautiful are you?

The path of beauty heralds the embrace of the sacred and feminine side of human nature. This feeling aspect is present in all people, regardless of gender. At this point in our collective and cultural evolution, the "return of the feminine" is widely regarded as quintessential to our next evolutionary step. The patriarchal system of the last few thousand years has served its purpose in bringing forth many important advances that may not have otherwise occurred. It enabled the development of agriculture, the founding of cities, the development of institutions, and the rule of law. But we are entering a new dawn of the human race where new qualities and organizing/disorganizing principles are required. Central to this is a return of the feminine and the sacred in all of us; and at the heart of the feminine is the re-emergence and also the re-valuing of Beauty, Goodness, and Truth. These are the very qualities that lie at the heart of the return of Sacred Commerce. Integral to this rebirth is a new kind of chivalry, represented by the Knights of Commerce. The new chivalry is none other than that of the Knights of the Round Table in modern form. Each knight embodied a specific quality: honor, loyalty, nobility, virtue, grace, trust, courage, courtesy, gallantry, authority, service, or humility. The sum of all of these twelve frequencies creates the resonance of chivalry. Pick one of these qualities to focus on each month, and just see what happens to the overall quality of your life.

And yet there is even more. The application of the deep feminine in the form of truth, beauty and goodness in action in the world leads to something even greater; and that something is actually a Someone. Even as our deepest spiritual aspirations draw us into Faith, Hope, and Love, we can't stop there, because even these virtues simply become another religious system – and we just become cogs in that system. No, the ultimate way to live Truth, Beauty, and Goodness – the ultimate way to live Faith,

Hope, and Love – is to live it as a person in a relationship with another Person – the one who is at the very centre of these virtues themselves.

For the eternal verities are not ultimate realities; they point to that which is beyond even them – God Him/Herself. As G.K. Chesterton said so aptly, "God is not a symbol of Goodness; Goodness is a symbol of God." Each member of this trinity is a symbol, a signifier which tells us something about God. This is the true reason we should pursue them and draw them into our lives. God, then, is not Beautiful—God *is* Beauty. All that is beautiful somehow reflects Him/Her. It serves as an icon, a doorway for us to walk through to the wordless, formless Beauty which is beyond all earthly forms and yet, paradoxically, is not separate from them.

Today's Knight of Commerce, then, knows that Heaven and Earth are one and the same; just as s/he knows that form and the formless interpenetrate each other and are one and the same. S/he serves something infinitely greater than themselves, greater than anything that can be given a name; yet at the same time he or she is completely at home in the everyday affairs of human exchange and interaction. S/he knows that we are all in this together, that nothing is separate from anything else, and that, therefore, everything – every word, gesture, transaction, thought and feeling – matters.

Today's Global Citizens recognize this time as the age of party-cipation, in which everyone plays a part and everyone is invited to thrive, to learn, and to grow into God together. Like the man or woman who has been "born again," the new Global Citizen sheds his or her old skin – that me, the first primitive individualism that was useful for a time – and is reborn a new person who recognizes their intrinsic unity with everyone and everything that lives and breathes.

In this new Age of Party-cipation we come to God with eyes and hands open, ready to dive in up to our elbows if that is what is needed. We don't have to sit in a cave for thirty years to become enlightened. We can do it here, right where we are, in the modern marketplace, as we learn to activate a true partnership relationship with the Divine. Our calling now is to be co-creators; co-creators with each other, but co-creators above all with God. We are finally entering the era of spiritual adulthood. What a joy and a privilege it is to have been born to party-cipate in this remarkable time! And to witness the birth of a new humanity.

Printed in Great Britain
by Amazon.co.uk, Ltd.,
Marston Gate.